Welcome to The Hotel Architecture

D1603452

Writing **Architecture**

A project of the Anyone Corporation

The MIT Press Cambridge, Massachusetts London, England

Welcome to The Hotel Architecture

Roger Connah

Library of Congress Cataloging-in-Publication Data

Connah, Roger.
  Welcome to the Hotel architecture / Roger Connah.
       p. cm. — (Writing architecture)
     ISBN 0-262-53153-4 (pbk. : alk. paper)
    1. Architecture. I. Title. II. Series.
NA2500.C597 1998
720—dc21   97-47324
                                                                CIP

For Elisabeth, by whom
Nadezna Alice, for whom

Part Three: *Welcome to The Hotel Architecture*

Part Four: *Ditto! Architecture*

Foreword

Welcome, indeed.

With considerable powers of verbal seduction, Roger Connah lures us into what seems a highly amusing and entertaining hell. Be warned: it is only after a while that we notice how closely it resembles the world of our everyday, and by then it is too late. Ensnared in his fable, we gradually discover ourselves, and this is less than amusing, given what we find. Complicit in his game, we cannot gracefully withdraw. The most, and the best, we can manage is the same sort of ironic laughter that many of Dante's contemporaries must have mustered in defense of self-respect after reading the first edition of the *Divine Comedy*.

But our author's goal, I believe, is not simply to skewer the phony, the pretentious, and the disingenuous, any more than to flatter the righteous, if they are anywhere to be found. Rather it is, as he implies clearly at the outset, to broaden the impact and deepen the bite of critical writing. This can only be done by lifting it out of the increasingly claustrophobic confines of academic argumentation and professional self-reference, by diffusing it into a semblance, an analogue of the familiar, the anonymous Hotel in which we transients are all registered, and from which only a few will voluntarily check out.

The move from the dialectical to the allegorical is in itself a highly critical one. Mired in obscure and turgid discourse, or swept along by flash floods of celebrity, even the most gifted architects today become prey to the vagaries of fashion, and their best works often little more than fashion's most spectacular examples. By becoming a poet and a fabulist, Connah invites architecture to join the fabulous landscape of the everyday, from which it derives its legitimacy and authority, and by which it obsessively justifies its machinations. That architecture then finds itself on a landscape of hellishly Boschian complexity and, at the same time, hellishly Kafkan confinement is no excuse for missing the fun or avoiding the hits. Life is mostly tough and reflection mainly and painfully self-revealing.

In this epic work, Roger Connah has turned criticism on its head, opening up a new set of critical possibilities that I hope others who aspire to a new understanding of architecture will exploit as ruthlessly.

And just in time for the millennium.

Lebbeus Woods
Vico Morcote, 14 March 1998

Acknowledgments

Acknowledgments are due the following organisations, universities, institutes, and events that have helped during the development of *Welcome to The Hotel Architecture:* Anywhere (Barcelona); Film and Arc, Graz (Charlotte Pockhacker); The Architecture Centre, Vienna (Dietmar Steiner); CAYC, Buenos Aires; CICA, Los Angeles; Hamburg Chamber of Architects (Ulrich Schwarz); Vilnius Contemporary Art Gallery; Tampere School of Architecture (Juhani Katainen); California College of Arts and Crafts; SAFA, The Finnish Association of Architects (Vesa Peltonen); and finally, more recently, the Department of Architecture at Cornell University. I would like to thank the latter for the possibility of presenting some of these lines and ideas during the Preston H. Thomas Memorial Lectures 1995 (a series of annual lectures supported by Leonard and Ruth Thomas in memory of their son Preston H. Thomas, who was a student of architecture). Thanks go especially to John Miller, Amy Cash, John Zissovici, and Val Warke.

Personal thanks for passing (by now possibly even forgotten) encouragement and interest go to: Mona Martin, Bertel Stenius, Dave Topham, Angus and Patricia Glennie, Karen Geary, Norma Wagner, Birgit Seissl, Ann Twiselton, Otto Wiesenthal, Peter Herbstreuth, Patrick Mazéry, Peter Kuglstätter, Gautam Bhatia, Bhuvan Lall, Amitav Ghosh, Hannele Pöysa-Mikkola, Tarja Virtanen, Leevi Lehto, Kari Kuosma, Eeva-Liisa Pelkonen, Antti Veltheim, Ignasi de Solà-Morales, Bernard Hafner, Volker Giencke, Wolfgang Feyferlik, John Ashbery, John Hejduk, Bruno Zevi, Dennis Sharp, James A. Sterling, and Timo Penttilä.

I would also like to thank my editors Cynthia Davidson (Anyone) and Roger L. Conover (MIT Press) for their enthusiasm to follow this project through and their unflagging desire to see the boundaries of writing and architecture extended.

On the verge of evening, nobody asks the dark
where it came from or who it is.
Edmond Jabès

The further we advance into the future, the
greater becomes this legacy of "antimodern
modernism."
Milan Kundera

Who is it that says most? which can say more
Than this rich praise, that you alone are you?
William Shakespeare

Preface: Naive Before the Subtlety of Charlatans?

Who is it that says most? which can say more
Than this rich praise, that you alone are you?
And where do we attempt to settle the score
But the blurb, gingerly edited for more than the few?
Architecture races ahead leaving less clues than ever
To those followers caught out on the windy limb
And others, desperate to untie the knot, may sever
Any resemblance that remains, that looks back to hymn
The praise of inflected sensuality. For those alone now
Lifting grace into unexpected domain, you are but a brave
Lost meaning leased out to the well-intentioned Tao
Of Architecture making its slow way back to Plato's cave.
    Who is it that says most, when this says enough
    And the rich praise diverts more intelligent guff?

Two events occuring around ten years ago began this long poem.
I was invited to a seminar in Helsinki on *Heroes and Architecture*.
The subtext was: Were heroes necessary? It was assumed that I
would be present even though I was living in India. Just before I
was to depart on an Airbus from Delhi I found myself marooned
in another city. I believe it was in Bangalore, though now I think
it might have been Madras. It was raining, and melons strewn
across the road were being crushed by the wheels of huge reckless
trucks. The squelch was deafening. Realising I would not make
the seminar, I decided to abbreviate my paper as a poem and fax it
to Helsinki. The first theme emerged: the idea of an architectural
paper as *poetry*.

Some short time later I found myself in Sofia with a mere
walk-on role in the UIA Congress. On the second day I was asked
to step in at the meeting of the International Critics of
Architecture (CICA) for an absent colleague. I had an hour to prepare a paper on fashion and architecture. I remember discussing
Edmund Leach and Lev Vygotsky and trying to reword ideas that
had been with me for years with no chance of exit. I also remember being confused by the emerging carnivalesque in architecture,

especially postmodernism and the burgeoning conference and seminar circuit. The second theme was born: the idea of the *Carnival in Architecture*. Increasingly, this Carnival was to become for me something that could not only operate under its own rules but could alter those rules as it proceeded. Architecture was suddenly very fluid.

Over the next ten years various conferences were offered up, especially after the publication of my first book, *Writing Architecture*. Each event seemed like a simulacrum of all the previous symposiums, albeit with a change of face, guard, and podium geraniums.

Repetition gained ground, not only in architecture but in my work and life. And though I sometimes could not differentiate the intellectual and moral passion from the inevitable showmanship, I was reluctant to let go of all meaning. I could hold onto my presence (or absence) only by turning to poetry. I had the idea of poetry of a deaf soul, meaning mine. Delivering symposium papers in verse then took over. The third theme, of a conference called *Ditto*(graphy), emerged and the poem began to take shape in an anti-epic style. One such symposium took place in Barcelona, where *The Hotel Architecture* was born.

Why is my verse so barren of new pride?
So far from variation but not quick change?
Re-enchantment I fear can no longer be put aside
Nor though is radical loss of geometry so strange.
Architecture is a battle royal certainly that none can win
Unless in the Hotel Lobby, the Last Architectural Hero
Out to impress, swerves then salutes the immortal kin
And plumps once more for the discipline's Degree Zero.
For me though it's on, the adventure calls, the Irish bull
And an obstinacy to resist, never quite to talk a good game
Until wearisome or whatever, maybe brinks to the full
And a new vocabulary trips, then gains in gentle fame
    For that is all but which a Bull carries and has carried.
    An Architecture to non-meaning, so deftly, so slyly married.

Naive I suspect I have been, but is this not understandable before the subtlety of charlatans, hijackers, surfers, and thieves? Nothing could be more significant and appropriate to the Digital Lounge, down the long corridor to the Imperial Ballroom, than the millennial banter of change and hope in architecture. Nothing was more natural than a hotel called *Hotel Architecture*. Certainly you can check out any time you like, but in fact you can never leave.

Welcome to The Hotel Architecture is a continuation of my own attempts at *writing architecture*. It begins in free form as it discusses the thrill, promise, and fetish of language and philosophy. The subject is philosophical hijack and the architectural bull. It seemed obvious, at least to me, that as the conductors of chaos grew in influence and architecture searched for a tight rationale beyond geometry, the poem should seek another dialogue in the interstices of architecture and meaning. It began to dodge between sonnets, songs, odes, and rhyming couplets, coinciding in recent years with that special contemporary mirror-moment when the architectural world came *face to screen* with Dittography. The poem, thus, became a critical adventure in writing as it tried to keep up with, to challenge, and to spar with the tactics and ethics of the architectural profession.

Writing and *Architecture* share habitual concerns. It might be that a less orthodox approach can reveal to us advantages in an otherwise obscure domain. It was Marguerite Duras who said of Georges Bataille: "His work gives error—broadly understood—the greatest chance." I wanted to give error in architecture a similar chance. This is not to say that clarity matters less in architecture than it does in writing. But it might be that the habitual concern for meaning that presides too wearily in architecture, and has done so for many years, leaves only something like poetry capable of taking "error" on. Language and discourse in architecture, the *archobabble* it has become, will never fully illuminate architecture, nor should it.

However clumsily and unworthily, I share with Bataille a stumbling, stuttering way of not really writing as I write. I am also not against architecture that has managed to write itself against language. If words die on us, meaning follows and architecture trails. So much better then for rebirth. Criticism and the architectural bull, gentle or less gentle contradictory forms, need to divorce themselves. Nothing else will do. We should meet architecture as we meet language, in the lobby, in the corridors, in passing. *Welcome to The Hotel Architecture* is an anti-epic that suggests there is more privilege in architecture than just being around and seeing out this millennium.

Undress ourselves to undo architecture? It is more than an undoing. "Subtle in interpreting experimental data," Primo Levi in *The Mirror Maker* leaves the same question for us as he left for the illustrious physicist's validation of telepathy, precognition, spiritualism, astrology, and psychokinesis: "naive before the subtlety of charlatans?"

Farewell Hotel, thou art too dear for my possessing
And like enough thou know'st not thy estimate.
So try, try and exit these words of scant finessing
Before the screens arrive, so provocative, so determinate.
And if you too have more than words out loose
Or have dangled language from out the bleak corridor
Remember it's only you that prepares the noose
And only you that stumbles feint at that horrid door
Through and down which descend, descend only on digital ways.
Let the sonnets boom, the odes range (*phew*) helter skelter!
Let the century rewrite and be rewritten in this craze.
For the millennium dome, doom and philosophical swelter
    Must annoint all, clutch and cling, those architects so cool
    That you alone in movement need pass the swimming pool.

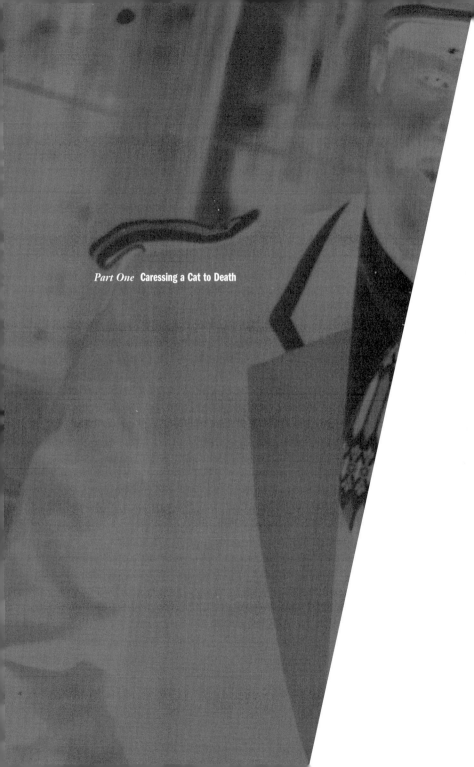

Part One Caressing a Cat to Death

one **Julio's Garden**

Caressing which cat to death?
How we like to pretend our disguises are safe
Doomed as they are in their touching appeals for authenticity.
Yielding as they do
            To the poetic in their wishful thinking.
And what for? An escape from eventual enigma?
Oh Incomprehensibility,
You give to the ultimate Bottom-liners their Mission.
Oh Tradition, response and genteel assimilation.
Stroking the cat on the return journey in order to announce

We were there. From the beginning. We were there.
Alert. Clever.
Much wiser than our work
Much wiser than our words. The head, after all these years,
Still considerably faster than the hand,
Always seeking the unreachable. The Unwritable.
Always about to say: We were there, yes, we were There!

But it's far too early to tell.
Too early to surf with Heidegger into Julio's Garden
Too early to vogue across the floor. But sooner or later
· · · ·
Followed by those four dots,
Trailing but not yet wonderfully uninterested
Leading us onwards to World Architecture.

Oh Fortuna! It is that simple
As we all enter another brief strategy,
Calling on an equal number of Contemporary
            And Not-So-Contemporary heroes
To enter with them into gentle oscillation
The attractive swerve and error of Architecture
            As the Carnival calls it.

And how
It rolls
It smacks the lips.

Oh Gentle Oscillation! Pleased with itself for repetition
Architecture stutters, breaking walls and wind.
Not unlike the authenticity of jargon
But oh so hard to make out, the jargon of its own
Authenticity wavering.

The Latecomers enter
Trailing, too, at first. But the era,
Some say a World Historical Situation,
Will see to the Carnival. Where it comes from.
Where it's going. And language
Left lying about in the corridor?
Just a hunch though
Where it learnt the privilege to speak.
To what purpose? And for whom?

Architecture, that tango to eternity? Let's run ourselves in,
Let's get close to those jugglers with history.
For every Kind Era, Echo, Candlestick
            There's a Valet, a Cough Drop, and a Bucket.

            And
Through the first gate into the garden, a beggar
Whose sloth of rare qualities delivers him from a world of fools
    and dupes
From a world about Renunciation. A correct world about
    authenticity
About caressing a cat to death, a beggar
Knowing more than all undecidable confrontations we can
    invent.
Put your tongue away, the beggar says,
Even these lines need their heroes for an efficent rehearsal.

And putting your tongue away, the Kind Era offers two options:
It invites our praise, or that velvet opposite, reproach.
It dumps on us or it embraces us
With the deaf poetry and curved venom of an architectural soul.
This will go on, few of us really need telling,
Until someone somewhere just cannot resist it.
They will shuffle the new cards into an eloquent tarot of
  generalities
Abstractions.
      A Tarot of Architectures!

The Kind Era, The Echo, The Candlestick, The Valet,
The Cough Drop, The Bucket.
One of them
      A sloth of rare quality perhaps
Will surf with Heidegger.
Or, more cautious, put an unlimited number of monkeys
To work on the word processor until they come up with the right
  lines.

        For example:
We must not believe, when we make a few discoveries, here and
  there
That this will go on forever
. . . .
Followed by those four dots again.
Even the monkeys will not be allowed to leave the Garden until
                Sooner or later,
The Idea is found and they get it right . . .

      Here it comes
Shall we follow?

Man everywhere encounters the illegible.
And who amongst us, cleverer than our work,

Cleverer than our writing, cleverer than the Kind Era,
Will pause long enough to dwell in this garden?

    El enigma de la realidad!
Miguel Cervantes, Ferdinand de, De Chirico, Jack Naipaul
               Or Julio Dali?

two **Sooner or Later**

Let's try another entrance into the Garden.
Let's rescue the cat from all those fundamental mysteries
Existential cores, and unique confrontations
        Oh, the authenticity of Jargon!
We must apportion blame
        The Carnival demands it
Nothing less is expected of us,
        Bottom-liners, possessors of innate sensibility,
Our Emancipators, dialling and punching cliché
To keep us walking
     Unblinded by insights
To keep us stumbling
     Towards the edge of the stage
No Lear to tell us otherwise, no card in the pack to fall out, no
  Hierophant.

Baseless Archobabble!
The poetic images in architecture are returning.
The mother of lonely utopia restrains itself;
              Rebirth is assured,
Or so we are told against the cards
Admirable restraint our lesson now,
        Not excess.
And Usurpia, awful word, its understanding assumed
When free of oscillation, seeks inspiration in the goodness of soil

In the Constructed Word.
Architecture undoes itself in the highway.
No longer self-portraits but artists!
     Restraint begins slowly, trying to explain the quasi-problems
It begins caressing its own cat to death.
     No longer between the lines but a thick brush
A zigzag downwards, a straight erasure and a raster overlay of
     doubtful brilliance,
     As thick as paint at the edges.
Gone now are the gentler sequences, the worrying perfection,
     violated by that little hop
     Skip and jump into nonfigurative tyranny.
Discourse bends and swerves, these triple limits
     That build up just when your back is turned.
The security forces massing in the shadows,
     Facing the other way,
They threaten to take on a life of their own
     In an era of their own, turning into a century of carnival
     distress.
And exhibitionism, forbidden any other description but
     Architecture.

three **Frenchman, Fire First!**

Authenticity. Jargon. Obfuscation. Rumour. Gossip. Eternity.
London. New York. Paris. Buenos Aires. Vienna.
The Capitals of the world's language.
The Capitals of the world's prisons.
Be there in a Tokyo minute. No, a Krakow minute!
It's a different game here,
The Carnival like polo.

How can one not surf unerringly at least once this century?
Guest Speaker asks. And it's printed:
To Err

Is an irretrievable part of the Carnival
Its introspection makes shamans of us all.
Few variations.
Little difference.
No vertigo!
But Architecture wants more than his vocabulary
Architecture wants his Word's world
And wants his attic on the outskirts of Paris.
A wretched garret with a garden and an orchard.
Architecture wants also the telling but unfair anecdotes
Surely the computer can be padlocked? No further access
And an Architecture kept in raging anarchy!
It is that simple, the Guests say. He has fooled us.
Errors are never unreasonable, only attractive.

But he's alone!
            They allow him not such slippage
And the Carnival wants what it needs not,
                  Language left lying around
        In a space
Where grids rotate, columns skew, light collides
And Carnival Architecture undresses like a soldier's whore.

The Carnival doesn't stop there. It disembowels.
It dismembers its own society. Counter-memory,
It decomposes into another language.
Yet another rehearsal of this century's loose eminence is violated
But gains membership of the Club: the Verbal Impairment
  Community.

The Irretrievables meet inside the Garden, next step the foyer.
Groucho knocks on the window of World Architecture
                  With a sponge dipped in neon.
Slow membership of the era,
Even slower withdrawal.
The Unavowables make up horrible words

That teach us how to dwell on ground but not soil,
Which cannot support itself.

They succeed
They tell us all this and more.
How to suck prawn and construct theories. How we should
   listen.
They've undressed everything and left the Kind Era seductively
   revealed.

And for what?

We are quicker now. But have we warned ourselves sufficiently?
We follow when we need. We steal words and usurp.
We disfigure ourselves. History vogues, for example,
Across the floor. A vague trocadero. Language
Once again a passenger to truth, opts out.
Apparently some cajoling, some moving errors, move even
   further,
Reaching as they do the suburbs of the globe.
The rotated axis, the punched plane, the penetrating diagonal
Will rewrite World Architecture soon enough.
Brutish geometry with a kind order, necessary but alas
   insufficient
                    To caress the cat.
The Carnival Whore fights for a dignified death.
Undressing space, language battles but remains inhabited
Long after the awards are made, long after the symposiums
   analysed
For their summertime gains by the up-and-becoming.

Oh Usurpia! They rush to hush
The Constructed Word as it is whispered in the suburbs.
For the future of Architecture

The Tarot pack reads: The wisdom of uncertainty
Disembowelled into joyous, carnival code.

four **The Hierophant**

Frenchman?
He did. Fire first.
He did. Err.
Contestation. Interrogation. Reformulation. Architecture,
The Hierophant decides
    As much by its substance, as by its form,
Is disembowelled by its word play. Less of those *glissements*
  progressifs,
    More an upset of Logocentricity;
Even if the Hierophant speaks of Architecture
    Language never belongs to it.

Did you say that on purpose?
They ask without interest
Are we to follow,
    Or reconcile ourselves among the stars?

  Cut-back?
    Cat-back
Thinking Architecture to stray down on us.
Bend to us, Oh Meta-Grumblers!
      And a few rise from their chairs, unhappy in the wrong
  script.
Passion lost, jealous fresh.
Oh Lonely Episteme
Now a new member of the Club, The Unavowables.
Terrible word, of course, that goes without saying.
Alterations have to take place in the tarot pack.
The instability of the Unkind Era has wasted ridiculous
    Sad time

Since way back when 1922 slowly rotated
         And suggested permanence.

Any seconders? they ask.
The Hierophant heightens the Carnival as trivially obvious
   architecture
Gains the authority of incoherence. Incensed enough to remain
   quiet,
Those lacking the agony of vocabulary are put up against the wall.
         Shoot first, interrogate later.
New Select Committees form.
Academies boogie!
Professors mumble; only corruption is stable.

   We knew. It did. It was.
And the cocktail partygoers pause, mingle, whisper:
         Dim light
      Space of disaffection
Radical!

But it's no longer convincing to recognise the pain
With which they fail to suffuse their words with meaning.
They retire, still expecting the Hierophant to pronounce
The Truth of Architecture. That favour passes over
To the newer intelligence agencies. The codes are undressed,
   then regarbed.
Unrecognisable now in the evening light
They turn anti-shadow into transient beauty
Falsified again and again by visual compulsion and poetry.

               The Hierophant surfs with Heidegger
World Architecture
            We are told
Can only ever be a silent articulation.
Not unlike then, punching a diagonal past
Through an English Cathedral, as if one represents in philosophy

The four trailing dots in architecture
. . . .
Whatever could they mean?
Filled with Others' fancies, empty of Others' meanings,
The Hierophant alters his tweed.
The buttons not quite aligned
He reads but doesn't want to: Disembowellism's future is
Constipation's past.
Which seems to the audience,
      Buttons perfect on its uncrumpled linen jacket,
Like killing your friend so that your enemy may survive
      Once again for you to hate; one more time
A paradox beyond the audience too.

But all too far into the garden, all too far this century to be pulled
  back
The Carnival writes itself out before it takes place.
      Silent,
Le mot-mode, simulacra, takes its place in the New World's words.
The Hierophant itches, shifts faster than the fetish and the
  dictionary.
Not, as some think, to keep up. But
To stay lost.

five **The Fool**

Sooner or later, we cannot delay it any more
Men and bits of paper, language still too attractive for poetry.
Perhaps then our new hero would write architectural sonnets
Not aphorisms. Our new hero, the Last Architectural Hero,
Would swerve as the Dodgers and Disembowellists do:
Just elegant Architecture
Underwear in the refrigerator.
That sort of chilling thing!
Inaction with fireworks . . .

Whilst amongst the heavy curtains
At the Teatro Cervantes
Carnival madness writes architects into an ineligible community:
Zero membership and maintenance.
The Museum of Disasters disperses them,
The audience dissembles them, the world dismantles them.
And other worlds pick up where they left off
At only a slightly slower pace, making up for the hasty errors
Or so we think. Architecture like language
                    Slewed again.

A tarot move of undecidability. The tower precious, the fire
    prepared
The stack of cards toppling. Nevertheless the party goes on.
The Insurance Agent smiles: These are the risks we have to take.
And it will take place, the Agent explains, in the unbuilt, the
    unfinished
In the indeterminate lobby of the Five Star Century Hotel
    Architecture.
The atriums lit with halogen trip wire
The herring bone in the tweed
And the fine concrete picked out like stringy veal.
The crystal service set amongst the dust and rose leaves.
The carpets coded with disc
Just in case Architecture doesn't materialize.
(*We know about the floppy shift in language*, the Agent booms!)
And our vocabulary has been nothing if not eminent.
We are now less sure
Of those caressing us towards more End-of-the-end theories.

The Fool, the card the Agent chooses . . .
But no one rushes to explain
Another of those usual predictions, another rewrite of the Kind
    Era.
If only this time, this time, Architecture could be fully achieved.
The reason is given and, if only momentarily, architecture
    survives

Then to shatter, to fragment, apparently once and for all.
Such joy is expected in an authentic chaos, in an archeological
   frivolity.
The Johnny-come-lately architects arrive.
Knowing Michael gives way to Knowing Peter
Which in turn skews to knowing Frank.
REM is not only Random Eye Movement.
The juke box has a twist of lemon, an olive
A dash or two. Nobody is caught voguing anymore across the
   floor.
It upsets the camera.
Everything, the Insurance Agent says, *like a lost mystery*.
Is this Archobabble or the wrong metaphysics?
Monsters emerge, Philip!
Check the frequency, Kenneth!

And there are those momentary lapses like Russian dachas
In the ruins of English cathedrals. Not democracy. Not
   mobbocracy.
Not ghettocracy. Not plutocracy. The Kind Era rewrites even
   race
And the depreciating legacy of mediocracy.

Oh *Fortuna*!

six **Temperance**

Is there a name for this?
Or a little Think-Cervantes, to sum it all up for us.
So neat at identifications these days, must we bother?
For as those exit from the Carnival
Other parties begin in on the chandeliers
The velvet curtains and other unfinished schemes.
More sit down, heads together;
The pose of eternity pondering the pagan once again
Juggling nomenclatura and the tarot members

Reintroducing Ferdinand de and where he went wrong,
Misreading Jean and forgetting Lev, manhandling Julia, and
   caressing Miles
Stumbling as the Carnival does
Across the fatal strategies
That threaten the wheelchairs of modern commerce.

And Architecture?
It's lonely up there among the Gods, the Seventh Dial
Where the heroes and promising authorities
Need pauses to free them from the advertising copy.
To free them from extending those dimensions that fettered
   them.
The advantage in insight only now plausible, Cervantes replies,
If it cancels out one's thinking.
This leaves us all miraculously balanced
Midcarnival, just arriving at The Hotel Architecture
Like a tarot card emptied of its neighbours, like words we cannot
   use again
Until the Idea is found, and the Kind Era exits the theatre.

      And when it does? you ask

When it does, the Garden is closed. The computer is padlocked
   from the inside.
Authenticity rewrites its own jargon
Dipping in and out of the halogen searchlights.
We will forget the Books on Laughter
And laugh at the Books of Forgetting.
The Invisible Cities will meet as their own secret community.

Inavowable, they'll be more stringent about entry.
Even Groucho would be denied random access as pessimists
See language reduced to favourite words. This time, *Simulacra*
Next time, *Maradona*. A football match at La Bocca,
A riot and a modern novel.

Exercises and rehearsals are echoes
For those in the surburbs of the globe, in Solitude
Where someone inhabits an Architecture
Invented only by images and memories,
        Instead of the genius we inhabit inside our dreams,
Armed with explosive *Semtext*.

seven **Death**

And our Johnny-come-lately architect?
What is he doing now? Rumour, eye movement, and simulacra
  have it
Commissioning has taken place. A small supplement to achieve.
An addition in the City of Nizam, for Lord Gale and Zara.
The first sketches are complete but violated in their fragments.
Desperate to echo the origins of the Carnival, Theory is never so
  desperate.
The Promising Architect is lifting the interior
To announce the intolerable heaviness of low ceilings in such
  clime.
The Promising Architect has, and knows it,
Become nothing more than the Dabble card. But it's a new tarot
  move
Extending the axis mundi to take in the Indian sky at night
Picking up fatal memory and resonance
Of a not-to-be-forgotten Raj.
                Elephant height!
The outer wall is punctuated
With an unwilling colonnade crashed through the natural stone
In another bid to write out the four trailing dots of Architecture

. . . .
The Constructed Word? The result?
Rumour, eye movement, and simulacra lied. No commission.
But beyond the Carnival there's no time to be lost

Footsteps are heard a little too heavily, a little too dramatically;
The tables are being prepared for the new guests
The crystal service replenished. Atriums lit. The new writers of
   the New Era
Will build monuments again.
And there's a relief in the breathing, the collective breathing.
Like that of athletes knowing that to go the whole way
They need to excell. If they do, the World knows their name
If they don't, Migraine. Still invited to follow?

Oh Teorema! Shall we?
      Apparently to some it comes easy, this excellence.
The tables are relaid, the space layered, the lyre ready. A few
   salty herrings
Prepared and packed in Iceland remind us
Of those lands smeared with a Land That Is Not. Architecture

Faceless. Guileless. And cleverly the region reduces itself again
To its minimalist death. The Bell ringer informs us of the
   embarrassment.
It's these Anglo-Saxon aspirations;
      How close to the life-saving science we really are.
You interrupt, can't hold yourself back.

I smile. I am famous for it. Like the Bucket-and-Spade card
To know and read the signs is no longer enough:
The young Modern girl, the one who should come through the
   forest,
Through the Hotel, as through these lines and take us to
The Land That Is Not, the young Modern girl is rereading *The
Magic Mountain.*

And us? We keep arriving. Not a Mann, not a Gombrowicz
Amongst us. We keep surfing with Hegel or Heidegger;
Cleverer than our own work.
      Cleverer than our writing, certainly.

Doomed to this joyous oscillation.
Doomed to this safe carnival like useful sex.

Architecture and the Garden?
An exit of exits. A place where the robe is pulled over the beard.
Backwards.
The Guests say we are not in agreement. There are others
  though.
Others who run with the surfers
In gentle incomprehensibility.
They construct words to live in, Architecture to write
And space to die, calmly.
                    In style.
World Architecture speaks now, the Carnival says
As if language were the question mark.
Architecture speaks, without interruption
Without small talk. Definitely no chat. Completely, imperfectly
  fragmented.

Caressed to death.

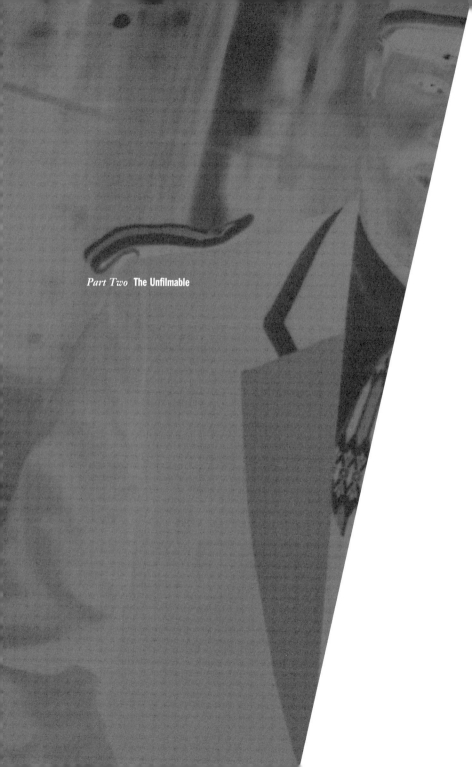

Part Two **The Unfilmable**

one **Architecture, Damn It!**

Listen without prejudice. Pick a card, Frank says
And your hand goes down for the last time. Out comes the card:
The Bucket-and-Spade card.
Frank reads it for you:
Architecture can't go on, it must go on, it will go on.
Meaning?
Meaning your suitcase is permanently packed.
Images Locked Open, the small print said down by the asterisk.
The invitation crashed through the door;
The Unfilmable was the title of the seminar paper.
Fortunately the carpenter had enlarged the letterbox
                    Before escaping with the caretaker.
It was all, how do they put it, politically dubious
            But the film they made of it years later won all the
      awards.

The Hotel Architecture,
      Like all houses,
                  Was wrapped on the outside in a blue translucent sheet.
Images played across its surface
      As a permanent tribute to Architecture's search for the new
      agenda.
Just like my house! Frank said, A holographic memory in ruins.
      But the landscapes ticked over
Virtually unreal before the robots even arrived.

Ladies, Gentlemen, time please, the Waiter interrupted:
                  Last orders for the New Millennium.

It had already been time
                  When you reached the cafe on the piazza outside The
      Hotel Architecture.
But then time has a habit, a nasty habit

Of mistaking probation for parole.
It has been Time for so long, then you die,
The Prize-winning Poet had said, receiving the cheque.
And no, I have no problem deciding what to do with my prize
   money.
Yes, it is really time now, the Prize-winning Architect said, and
   beckoned the Waiter.

Meanwhile, as the Illuminati embrace the Last Architectural Hero
You prepare a paper for another year's finance.
The topic: 'An unhysterical account of your own redundancy'.
The delivery: Stuttering and famous for it!
The application?

Dropped in the mail box in the lobby of The Hotel Architecture.
Dropped in the mail box marked 'Mail Box', Architecture yawns;
Stuttering and famous for it. Semiotics and its full catastrophe:
The Democracy of Sign . . . (never had it! never will!)
Stuttering and famous for it—Architecture, damn it!
Film and Architecture.

two **Postcard Pathologies**

Between the time it took the Waiter to come
You had written another pathology on a postcard.
Always bounded by ideas that are only attractive in their error,
You, like Architecture, turning yourself into an industry.
Outside on the Cathedral plaza, the hoops are set up for the
   skaters.
Everywhere the Powerbooks are left open,
Like Calzone cut at the throat.
Whilst in the kitchens at The Hotel Architecture
     The salads are tossed
     The omelettes are whipped

The steak is layered
The oregano over-applied

And Architecture prepares itself
        To be yet another supplement of Undecidability.

The skateboarders surf into the lobby of The Hotel Architecture
        On tilted planes locked inside unreal space. Nostalgia is
    upset.
Silent wisdom no longer results from lazy fascism as
        The Professors fight like bald men over the comb.
 And the parents of a Lost Architecture
        Mock this childless guise and guile.
The Powerbook stares back into their faces
        Notes are taken and read aloud into a screen.
The screen stares into its own space;
The surface is all we have.

It screams,
            It screams
So deep,
            So deep

The Skateboarders exit The Hotel Architecture in a hurry for the
    beach
They no longer hum the soundtrack of this century. Instead
They mime the firm zero we are all envious of—
You can check out anytime you like
But you can never leave.

Meanwhile, the Powerbook works without aids,
It writes itself into the history of this century's dreams as
Truffaut meets Lang in the lobby of Invisible Architecture;
In blank form, *Finnegans Wake* on its software.
Architecture, they stutter, is reprogrammable

Just as in Godard's reversible aphoristic world.
The moral . . .
> Ah the moral, Frank interrupts, impermeable
>
> . . . .
>
> Is in the travelling.

That's mine, Laurence Sterne says
> From the cloisters at Jesus College, Cambridge
As the director tilts to take in the oldest tree in the city

> . . . .

> Cut.

three **Reading the T-shirts**

Can you make a film from a postcard?
> Delaney, the Irish Police Chief asks.
But no one listens without prejudice.
And the real book of the Postcard remains unopened,
Wrapped like all buildings in its tough, glossy translucent cover,
Images playing across its emptiness!
Brought to book, you were, but they could never quite
Capture the suicide in all but the gentlest movement.
All applications for Architecture
To reach the next millennium were to be suspended.
'Take time out' is a phrase overheard, but so easily does it blur
That Overstretch becomes a theory all its own.
The Waiter arrived
> Finally!
It takes that long in The Hotel Architecture.
(It has always taken that long in The Hotel Architecture)
> But whilst Frank chooses the new colour scheme
Harry has upset the binoculars
Of our Last Architectural Hero.

The Waiter's pause indicated the type of world service
That needs no more explanation.
Concerned enough, though,
He did ask about Architecture's health.
On his face the crushing delight:
　　　We're all in this unrest together.
　　　You, me, Film, and Architecture!

Oh the Pathognomic! Frank says to Harry.
Harry was playing with his asterisks in a text as yet unwritten
In an Architecture as yet Invisible

READ THE T-SHIRTS
　　　STAY ALIVE
The Waiter's T-shirt exhorted
Whilst Da Vinci's Measure of Man became
Man's measure and flipped this century
　　　　　　　Into a romance with dimension
It could ill afford.

The advice came free with the shirt:
Advice Architecture could afford to take
As Frank began cutting up the menu into twelve equal parts
Reconstructing once more
Architecture's own attractive errors.

Deconstruction, forget it! Harry said,
We have always been more than a trend, haven't we, Frank?

Still, it was obvious if you happened to look around
And the blindness had not stuck that
There was no Time in any real sense left.
The auditorium doors had opened
Architecture was showing at the Hotel Cinema, Aurora.
There was panic all around.

Everyone was given laser spex.
(Look at a light. You won't believe your eyes—
But never look directly at the Sun!)
Sad, Frank said
What is? Harry asked
Architecture!

    . . . .

The three dots that divide all statements into sense
              And non-sense became four, once more
As Harry stumbled to find the peanuts dropped down the soft
  sides
              Of the velvet sofa.
Seasonally adjusted dementia became an alibi,
But the Waiter was onto this vacillation:
The World's architects had hung around the hotel too long,
Why should he replenish the peanuts and change the silver
  platter?

Lock up the images, the Waiter had rumbled the assembly,
Before you do more damage.
Before the Cinematographer arrives, you mean?
That was sharp of Harry, and the Lobby noticed.

The Waiter called Harry over
      Such a winning way about him, you had to agree.
But what could he possibly mean?
      And who had finished all the roasted peanuts?

If there was time and more than a short-term memory
      There would be an attempt to answer these questions,
But Architecture was impatient,
      Somebody has invented the word *Saussurization*

Written a book about it. And theories rolled out, overstretched,
　　Arbitrarily linked to the question of space,
To the run of peanuts down the velvet sofa. Crucial:
　　Architecture could no longer smile and be famous for it

With Harry's f-stop and steady-cam grin
　　The smile on Architecture's face had no chance.
Flaubert danced into the Lobby,
　　Recalled by the holographic memory, and began

Propounding the theory of the pace of society's yawn
　　And the frequency of smile.
But then smiles brought up in the wrong city,
　　Flaubert said (*unhappy with the nickname,*

All but ruined his chances for the Gold Medal!),
　　Smiles brought up in the wrong city, inhabiting the wrong
　images
Writing the wrong architecture
　　What chance did they ever have?

There was a pause in which another city
　　Vanished from the genomic Mental Map without trace.
Two lines sufficed where there should have been four,
　　But the drifting, the fidgetting continued.

There's no time to be lost, Harry said to Flaubert,
　　As if by acknowledgment the character would become real
And step out of the pages only to stumble Degree Zero
　　Pushing Architecture outside all.

Hurry, before the Cinematographer arrives from the airport,
　　Flaubert's last words trailed away.
Outside The Hotel Architecture, Architecture stepped over death,
　　Flicked the cigarette packet away with the right foot.

A neat flick! One which the gondolier might learn,
As he shouts to the canyon in Venice—'Storia! 'Storia!

. . . .

four **'Storia**

'Storia! The Gondolier repeats as
The homeless sleep over the metro grill and
The Prize-winners occupy the cinema unable to move,
Unable to respond to our Last Architectural Hero.

Why? Frank shouts in more voices than he thought he had.
Speaking for Architecture, a stranger replied:
It's warm, stupid, and there's such solidarity
In the unfortunate position.

Everywhere, announcements on the metro walls
Of the post-philosophical world where
The Book of Questions turns into the Question of the Book.
And the film of the Book of Questions

Turns into the Question of the film.
But as ever it is impossible to show the capital letters
In the oral exercise.
Down in the basement of the subway, the gay community

(*Is this it? These two?*) discuss the recent conference.
Their pronunciation has a paperback accent over the letter e.
'Storia, the gondolier shouts again, negotiating a sharp turn
As nostalgia is falsified. The corpse, reheated.

The plaza is full of umbrellas.
Only the film, *not* the architecture, Frank says, is ruined.

The music strains across the void.
    The Theologist sits on the piazza bench taking notes

For the next conference (working title) Dittography.
    On the juke box at The Hotel Architecture,
An old favourite. And, confused, the Prize-winners go for it:
    Here comes the sun, on a dark desert highway

The food is micro-live,
    The beer threatened only by other varieties
Not the price of oil. In The Hotel Architecture
    There is no let up in the silence

And the theories made over to how Architecture forms itself
    Time and time again
By a somersault over etymology and diacritics.
    And in the Question of the Book?

Someone, somewhere, anywhere
    Before the millennium is up
Buys one copy and copies the rest.
    Liquid space. Liquid sales. Liquid architecture.

five **Strangers in the Neon**

    So let's have none of this pain as text,
Harry says as the neon over The Hotel Architecture
    Comes on in the early evening.
There are, after all, less accusing fingers, less accusing cities.
    Electronics without prejudice, on the neon across the cathedral.
The entourage arrives from the airport
    Once a stranger, always a stranger in neon,
But the Cinematographer has great advantages.
    After all, Harry says and drifts away, unlike Architecture

He knows when to be a stranger to himself
    He knows when to let go, he knows—
        When to decide . . .

    Decide what? Frank asks, mind reading on behalf of the
  Prize-winners.
Just how much to edit out of the image,
    Harry replies,
Breaking off his cocktail stick from Fatal Airlines

    Seminar-ready for one of his lectures.
Like a city, Harry continues, the Cinematographer knows
    How much to edit out before it is inhabitable.
Like a world, the Cinematographer knows

    How much to turn before it comes to a standstill.
'Storia or hysteria?
    There was no stopping Harry now.
This leaves, he said, *your Architecture still wandering*

    The City of Cities. A delicate poetics of unrest,
If you like. But I've seen it all here in the Hotel.
    Everyone hushed, the joke box obeyed,
Harry had the killing floor to himself

    Always leaving language lying around in the corridor
Always expecting Architecture
    To open the locked images carelessly
Don't you ever realise?

    There was silence in three languages
Which in other parts of the globe
    Become theories of critical resistance:
Seduction of the predisposed, self-evident wisdom!

Sense and non-sense
All fight it out in the chiasma.
No one quite understood Harry's thesis:
But then no one should try.

Harry shared the obvious with the Cinematographer—
Never make a thesis from a story,
Build it as Architecture instead!
Take that, Last Architectural Hero, Harry says.

On cue, our hero took his turn.
Why do you stay here in the hotel then? Frank asked,
Wondering if Flaubert was back or then Cervantes
Would make the expected appearance

And just about carnivalise Architecture into the irretrievable.
There was, though, no sign of even a virtual Miguel de!
Go on, why do you stay? Frank was disappointed
That no digression could alter the discourse.

Because, Harry replied, Architecture still wants
To inhabit a dream that is yet to be performed.
The pin that dropped onto the walnut floor
Had more theories of architecture on its head

Than anyone dared contemplate.
Architecture stays because it can decide to go.
Put that on your T-shirt;
Harry finishes his lecture with the words
. . . .
And film it!
. . . .
Now cut!

six **Son of Aphorism**

No
Architecture doesn't stay for the cheap alcohol
Nor for the lenient motorway rules, nor for the f-stop.
No
Again no . . .
Architecture doesn't stay for the steady-cam smile
                    That swallows civilisation
For the seduction of the city itself
As it catches up with a world it once thought
It had long left behind.

Then why does Architecture stay at the Hotel?
The barricades were going up everywhere.
For every image we produce, Frank says, there are
                    At least two Presidents.
Reassured by this dazzling insight
The Prize-winners head for the barricades.
It's important, they say, echoing the wisdom of Smart Cards,
To lock up the image once and for all . . .

What chance the aphorism, then? Harry says
Looking up at the neon sign across the Hotel's two breasts
Designed in free-formed foamy beton brut:
Welcome to The Hotel Architecture.
Such a nice sign, such a nice line:
(Tilted and a slight jaded
After performing so long for television commercials,
For modern novels and footballers.)
What chance the aphorism when the T-shirt has taken over?

Harry breaks down having attempted all this;
Sensing something that comes to all of us—Delay.

(*Oh if we could but just*)
The Demolition Man enters this century right on time as
The Logics of Disintegration is deciding the Academy Awards and
The Logics of Respite builds nostalgia, whilst Son of Aphorism
Takes the new migraine treatment called Fortuna.

Oh Fortuna!

But it's too late
The T-shirt iconography has taken over
    Taxonomy first
        Scholarship later
And if you have to gossip
Then please, Son of Aphorism says, do it well.

It is a long time since you read the Invitation:
Your presence is required at The Hotel Architecture
A forum on film and architecture
We can offer a small honorarium
(*And we do need the younger voice amongst all these old Trots*!)

There was a pause in the Powerbook.
The battery remembered its half-stage.
And You, a half-life in words,
No longer interested in replenishment.
(*But could we ask you a favour*?) The invitation ran on—
We are in need of a little taxonomy of gossip, *oh and how*
The Net demands some architecture and tattle. *So could we?*
Just some thoughts, rapidly processed, anything will do. You see
We've not really had the time to think about it. But it's on our
    agenda.
Really anything will do. Surely you get around
Frequent flyer of Fatal Airlines
Surely you know what it is like in the lobbies of
All the Hotel Architectures around the world?

And really, we've not had the time. . . . But it is, yes

There's that word again, Time.
How it flatters your walk-on role this century.
How it flatters Architecture's walk-on role.
In the railway-station plaza there is an ethnic service
That prints Time on your own garments free of charge
(Like the old gangster joke—
You are my friend, I kill you for nothing!)
Architecture is your friend, it does it for nothing!

Or then a modest fee. But that's too late also.
A young skateboarder announces
            On a sign strapped to a sandwich board
The only conspiracy of hope left today
            Is beyond the aphorism itself.

The Lobby at The Hotel Architecture erupts, fragments,
                        Turns inside out.
Architecture is on the move again.
Re-Joyce, re-programme *Finnegans Wake* and Jean Luc Godard

The Moral . . .

Ah the Moral, just wait a minute,
            Laurence Sterne interrupts from
The cloisters at Jesus College, Cambridge
The moral . . . my dear forlorn colleagues, is in the Unrest.

No, Frank says, wishing Miguel de had appeared and not Sterne;
They order these things better in France.
They always have done. The Moral . . .
                        Is in the theatre.

The silence on the pin's head shifts axis
And writes another theory of Achitecture's import whilst
Only now it is being admitted that
The twentieth century has that known-variously disease:
Myalgic encephalopathy.
Shortened to ME: chronic fatigue, post-viral fatigue syndrome.

The moral is in the theatre, it always was and always will be,
                          Frank says
The theatre of world images!
Our Last Architectural Hero of the Century emphasises every
    word.

Meanwhile
The Seminar at the Other Hotel Architecture has been running
    on empty.
Conclusions are about to be made.
The panellists requested to make their way back to the stage,
The podium decked out in geraniums and dahlias.
What catastrophe for Architecture awaits
When Film begins to make sense of our dispassion?

Oh Digitial iconography
Oh Brutal disco
Oh Migraine
Oh Fortuna

It amounts to the same, Architecture says.
But where on earth can I find the new agenda?
The Director asks, as Harry enters with the final cocktail, the
    Bellini.

Locking the images open, Architecture escapes film.
The neon surfers skateboard into the cathedral square
        Only to discover in front of The Hotel Architecture
That they might not want to die in an image there.

seven **Scaffolding Anxiety**

Forget Life Insurance, Harry says, bringing the cocktail stirrer,
Forget Pensions. Harry stirs the cocktail.
Existential consolation in the locked image is no longer enough.
Rapid succession of unreal images has altered
The Hotel Architecture's decor faster than we expected;
The dynamic processes of film limp behind.
There's pandemonium. The human touch realises
Too late that Architecture has never been vast enough
To scaffold this anxiety.

The Cinema announces its contemporary response.
Medals pin the breast flesh back, Prize-winners take the cheques
Whilst underneath reveals the latest Metropolitan T-shirt.
A substitute for a telephone catalogue, the T-shirt reads:
Film the locked image open!

If language be your scaffold, then clamber, lightly
Ever so lightly.
Film is no match for language's fall.

Don't interfere, Frank says, Architecture never completes
   anything.
We saw that in the garden, we see it now in the Hotel, pull back.
But too late again, the theatre of world images lines up for
   penetration.

Well, Frank says, *you are all wrong, you, Flaubert and Sterne.*
They order these things better in Hollywood,
And at least they protect the bodies and the lens.

Harry had surprised Architecture with his one-liners.
He had rhythm if the others had not. He had—and he wasn't
   letting go—

Architecture under his skin.
Outside, always night, always bright but only 500 lux
Blue and green, the neon flashed across corporate-energy
  advertisers.
Suddenly a clear seminar thought entered the Lobby and
Crashed into the skull of The Hotel Architecture

Oh Fortuna! Lazy stray Cesna, get it out of here.
                    Yet it persisted:
Architecture writes itself against your will.
Architecture films itself against your thrill.

In a language wounded from lack of light
In Lands where the boundaries have always proved lonely
In Nations trapped in the dull theatre of world images
Just what is this and why do we have to appear so miserable?
                    Harry asks the Prize-winners.
Do we blame the Cinematographer or the Scriptwriter?
Frank speaks for Architecture
                    Whilst more tired barricades go up:

Do we all live in this theatre?
Are we all asked to perform for whims behind us?
For paradoxes beyond us?

eight **A Paradox Beyond You**

Now there's no time to lose.
For the sake of our agenda, the Parachutists remark,
We had to write you into the Architecture, then film it.
How were we to know about all this nausea?
What could we do with all this ME and chronic fatigue?
Who can blame the Producers?
The budget demanded action, Architecture responds.

WYSIWYG

Architecture has no choice. It anthologies itself
          Into newer and newer cultural movements.

You poured the mineral water left in front of you
Whilst the Chairman, Miguel de or Rafael, introduced you with
  the wrong name.
It seemed of so little consequence.
He knew neither whether Architecture drank its Bellini or its
  Rogers.
Your mouth opened anyway:
Creative boredom, even the Cinema, you said,
Has a century of putting to use our own emptiness.
There was silence all around. Nothing dropped.
Not even the pin,
Weighed down now with so much theory that history had been
  evicted.
Some other voice continued inside you:
Consider the soundtrack of the film to go with the last decade of
  the century.
There are options:
    Nothingness.
        Eat the Peach.
            Heartbreak Hotel.

It wasn't worth it. Harry brought the tray and the espresso.
Why can't you order a normal coffee? The Vampire said,
Grabbing hold of the Gold Medal Winner under the table
Whilst redesigning a meditation suite for The Hotel Architecture
                    To satisfy her own agenda.
Eat the undecidability of your heart out—
She continued in a jargon left over from her software—
The Museum of Modernism has paid for the installation,
    What do I care for the soundtrack of Architecture this
  century?

Harry, upset at this outburst, interrupted proceedings with
  dessert.
It was a small cassette. He played it.
More one-liners, impoverished rhymes for impoverished times:
A crime to dream!
A metropolitan to scheme!
An Architecture to glean!

nine **Chiasma**

Sense and non-sense collided. It was to be our greatest hope.
Our redemption. The Son of Aphorism was happier.
The Last Architecture Hero swerved into
              The Film of the Book, Architecture!

The critical discourse shot out on the hotel neon.
Electronic heaven, the Son of Aphorism fainted.
What was it like inhabiting an architecture in language
                      Without the support of any images?
Now he knew . . . But it was late down there in the Square.
The commerce begins. Cross-trading rampant;
Hard disks were being sold for exorbitant prices.
The Son of Aphorism decided to trade life for a T-shirt.

Ill-advised, Wisdom takes the return journey
Whilst those unlucky to be born with early wisdom
Remain unastonished, remain unmoved
Condemned to sit through the century's film all over again.

They have started reconstructing the cities buried in the last ten
  years
With their loose black clothes and short memory
Their gentle By-Pass opens up a brevity.
              Gran pregio, la brevità

The Powerbook is still in the kitchen
The Network is open, on line is such a fine line.
The screen has taken over from the scene
                    And crashes through the next narration:

No one dreams anymore of making any thesis from any story
WYSIWYG
A runaway film on the unastonishing implications
Of Genetic Engineering and Architecture

When astonishment . . . Well, frankly . . . Astonishment has
  buried itself.
The script continues: A detective hired by the architect
Takes the golf caddy and gets out at the water hole.
(*Catch an image off guard and what does it tell you?*)

Catch Architecture off guard and what does it tell you?
Return it. Watch it double itself like a bet on the green felt
As the sovereignty of film picks up on the return journey
And learns by heart the phrase: Unlock the images open,
Inhabit Architecture again before it is too late.

ten **Breathe**

Breathe . . .
And we all try whilst the Architects wear sweaters to let others
  know
Breath still comes in the usual sizes:
Small. Medium. Large. Extra Large. XXL. XXXL.
Don't fool yourself, Harry says,
I've been in The Hotel Architecture far too long.
It really is a little late to blame naivety
For all this early wisdom.
Call it unadulthood, why don't you

And while you're still at all this cleverness
Why don't you accept the thrill of unrest?
Yet where do we go from here? Frank says
Timid, self-satisfying, good form? The question trails off
. . . .

Always the Third Man seeking the image
Frank asks himself about Architecture,
                    Realising no one else has any answers.
What image? Harry asks
The image to inhabit.
The image that will desperately seek the codes
                    And the password it needs

Frank was pleased with his answer.
Architecture, Frank thinks but keeps to himself, is a scaffolded
    anxiety.
Probably due to the space and pace of all information, it is blamed
    on cinema.

Blame it on the unfilmable and the drab information highway,
Harry says,
Getting the point of all this rogue poetry and telepathy
                    And of course, the coats for the seminar guests.
The Unfilmable can always get away with it.
Like the perfect murder, it can lock up all the images open.

No clues for Architecture this century though, only films about
    the crime.
Not a change of vocation or commission for the unemployed
But definitely a means of fulfilling the loose hours
As a Software Negotiator or Mortuary Attendent. It's late.
The Seminar invitation lies inside the door. Why open it?

Who tells Architecture to walk and stop at the ditch?

Who tells Architecture to arrive at the enigma?

Who tells Architecture to stop at the supermarket freezer
                        Where you take a beer?

And from there Architecture is taught to waltz over to the meat
  counter.

Probably the best aphorism in the world that:

(*Film and Architecture*) Locking the Images Open

Or then:
                        Waltzing over to the meat counter!

eleven **Copyright in Dispute**
(courtesy The Eagles and The Lone Rangers)

On a drab information highway, cool waves in its hair
Warm smell of architects, rising up through the air
Up ahead at the Diagonal, we saw the fragmenting signs
Our ideas grew heavy and site grew dim
We had to deconstruct the lines

There it stood in the lobby
Sounding its decision bell
Architecture thinking to itself
This could be heaven or this could be hell
Then lit up its atrium and showed us the way
Seminars down the corridors
We thought it heard them say

Welcome to The Hotel Architecture
Such a lovely place (*such a lovely space*),

Plenty of rooms at The Hotel Architecture
Anytime of year, you can find it here
Any point to them

Architecture's definitely twisted, knows where displacement ends
It's got lot of pretty pretty boys, that it calls friends
How it flickers in the courtyard, sweet discourse bends
Some deconstruct to remember, some deconstruct to forget

So I called up Captain Frank,
Please bring us our wine.
But Frank said, *We haven't had that spirit here*
Since nineteen sixty-nine.
And still those discourses are falling, from far far away
Breaking up in the middle of the night
Just hearing themselves say

Welcome to The Hotel Architecture
Such a lovely place (*such a lovely space*)
Such a lovely place,
Living it up at The Hotel Architecture
What a golden prize, given to alibis

Mirrors in the ceiling, the Perrier on ice
Frank said, *Architecture's full of prisoners*
Left to their own device.
And in the Legend's chambers,
They gathered for the feast
Stabbing with their Art Pens
Just can't slay the beast

Last thing architecture dismembers,
            In the shuttle to Dum Dum
Had to find its passage back
            To the following Forum

Relax, said the Lightman,
Architecture's programmed a reprieve.
You can check out any time you like,
But you can never leave.

twelve **The Video Coach**

By now the Video Coach has arrived outside The Hotel
    Architecture.
It begins to take the trip offshore.
Watch the world close up
As the seat besides is occupied by a nervous Prize-winner.
                                  Where now and why?

The potted plants inside the coach are for the Academy of
    Architecture
Whilst the sun vacations down on the coast and abandons the
    city.
Film? At least it's an art that travels, the Coach Driver says,
Reminding you just how organised and ubiquitous
The One-liners have become. Architecture takes a seat on the
    luxury coach.
As it leaves the galaxy, the videotape is wedged inside.

Some passengers alight at Birmingham, some at St. Petersburg,
Others at Paris. The rest stay for the entire journey.
Passing landscapes of ruins,
Architecture catches the graffiti that can never be filmed.

> Aesthetic Intention: Gameboy
> Expressive Intention: Lego
> Existential Intention: Nail-biting

Three things, the promising architect Zara says as

They all climb aboard the Video Coach. But wait,
My son will put on the siren on his police car:
EEEAW . . . EEEAW . . . EEEAW . . . .
         Film and architecture?
Donkey business, let's send a postcard from the galaxy to Delaney
They say there's a cease-fire. It's permanent this time,
And the emergency cord is pulled by mistake.
The Bengali guard on the coach fires up.
He puts down his *Wittgenstein Reader* and catches the child in the
   eye;
The siren wailed as it has done throughout this century
Throughout this locked image
But there was no longer any sign of Flaubert or Ferdinand de.
. . . .

Landscapes passed

Landscapes of the violent soul which the cinema softened,
Splendid images, it has to be said, of doomed visions and lazy
   fascism
That has been known to be referred to as politics.
It's alright, Frank says, if Architecture is all inside out.
He spoke through the words like a reversible raincoat,
   impermeable.
Harry was still aboard the Video Coach
Serving drinks to the participants and Prize-winners.
Next stop: Promising Architecture!

But don't ever dream of writing words like that again,
Harry says.
Death today in tweed, not gabardine.

         Architecture and film?
Showerproof, all centre, no circumference.

It makes for good television though, the Media Officer says,
Good television, poetry, and culture.
The perfect cut-up and telematics in the airport.
As the Video Coach left, The Hotel Architecture receded in the
    distance.

We knew this was the solution. All of us,
But we couldn't quite picture it.
Then we lost interest in just about anything we had invented,
In any country we had lived in.
That, Harry said, was probably the next-best aphorism
                    Film has ever offered Architecture.

The Offshore Architects got off to check their accounts.
They were disappointed. In Birmingham and St. Petersburg
The cashpoints had been raided by heavy-duty trucks.
Hard Disks raped. Space Coordinators were everywhere to be
    seen
Unemployed from The Hotel Architecture chain.

Waiter, Harry tries, there's a space coordinator in my sushi.
What's she doing? the Bengali Guard asks right on millennial cue.
Coordinating space, Harry mouths, but there's no life left in the
    words.
The Video Coach dropped the party at Dum Dum airport.
No smoking
Whilst the crumbliest, the flakiest,
Lizard crawling, wonderful computer fidgetry
Writes on the wall in Architecture
That disappears as you enter it:

You'll never be the same again!

It's virtually a world, not a Virtual World.
These were probably Frank's last words as an Architect.
Environments perform for you at the touch of a button.
They say you get the images right if you try hard enough.
It is the same with film. These were Harry's last words as a
  Waiter.
Meanwhile, a stranger to yourself, you still ask
What are you doing here?
Today it's Electronic Confession time;
Father Interactive came to stay and sent you a gracious postcard
                    Analysing your pathology.

Film has never found Architecture easy, Father Interactive said,
Nor has it ever known where the image wanted to die:
At home or offshore on the satellite.
No lightness and unemployed ashtrays
Are going to caress film to death.
Father Interactive had shifted his language
Until he, too, joined the Parachutists.

    No one, just no one, talked human anymore.

Whose fault is it, you ask Father Interactive,
That Architecture has missed out on its own talent?
To miss the point of its own art?
Interrupting the net, Harry began to surf in the lobby of Dum
  Dum Airport.
The Book of the Film is what matters now,
Harry says, monitoring all the moves of all the electronic lizards,
Writing new graffiti to replace that erased from the world's
  subways.

No more The Hotel Architecture,
Full flavour, all centre, all edge;
Architecture answers to the copywriter's dreams.

Fortunately, Father Interactive says,
Film will never capture the centre of the word—
Only chocolate has that privilege.
But The Hotel Architecture had long been taken over.
The unemployed surfers and skateboarders squat
                In the comfortable sofas in the Lobby. Eyes glazed
They give offers for an image of the century;
Architecture still refuses.
But it's only a matter of Time.

Suspect, Architecture will never be the same again.

On the screen an advertisement:
For beautiful kitchens and bathrooms they recommend
A water resistant coat. Safeguard yourself, Father Interactive says.
Leave the thrill of this world:
Go for Kierkegaard.

Offshore, the Weather Forecaster failed.
The sweater belonging to a Prize-winning architect
                Ran in the machine and washed out the film.
Architecture could do no more
Than wish itself another good day.

Alas, the story that went wrong,
                The thesis that tripped on its own democracy:
Architecture wanted science but got cinematics instead.
'Storia or Hysteria, the Gondolier still shouts
Down the canyons of silence in Everyman's Venice.
Tears were breaking through happily to the other side of the
    locked images.
We were nearly there.
In fact there we were
Breaking through to all the locked images
Now locked open. There we were
In pursuit of the next Millennium
                And Super Mario.

Part Three **Welcome to The Holel Architecture**

You can check out any time you like
But you can never leave . . .

one **The Gardener**

Farewell to reason
        Welcome to The Hotel Architecture
We are, Mr Norton says,
        Staging the event of Architecture
As a performance. We will perform
        The symposium you are about to attend.

The dahlias sleep in an ephemeral promise
        Not of their own making
Whilst others dance around
        The simulated bonfire passing an orange
To each other, under the chin
        Waiting eagerly for the early foul and trivial reality.

What open field? The Gardener interrupts
        Don't speak to me of an era of *fortunate simplicity*
There is no such thing. Reality is trivial
        It always has been. The orange slips
And is awarded penalty points:
        Fair game or virtual unreality.

        Fuerza! Architecture we once put behind us
When we laid out pennies on the railway tracks
        To get the flattened but hot remains
Of once legal tender.
        Never solemn, we broke through
Holding Echo et al., each by the hand

        And don't give us yet another Degree Zero
To compensate for the stillness of your skewed world
        Displacement. Clear as a bell. Dung and death.
Those assembled a fraction early for the end of
        The Millennium in the lobby of The Hotel Architecture
Are astonished but have difficulty showing it.

The Gardener sighs, repeatedly but different.
Don't wait for the grand stolidity and heaviness
　　To come around once again and pray for lightness,
It's already too late.
　　Time cannot be finished on time
For the Group Photograph on the rooftops.

　　The Gardener looks up, takes a card from the pack.
I can see it from your fingers as it squeezes
　　The camera with more brains than is good for it.
All but the eager are ready to pretend you were there all along!
　　Out of the pack comes the Car Wash card
Unaltered for thirty years.

　　We are warned of the complacency that can entertain
Any style possible. Remember: Wash, go, and flow!
　　The Flat Tyre ladies laughed from the other room:
Did the Travel Agent plan this?
　　The chance to attend the fin-de-millennial symposium
On Dittography. Fly direct by Fatal Airlines

　　Pick up the frequent flying points.
Lord Gale looks on having skipped The Unfilmable
　　And gone straight for the Awards Ceremony in the
　Ballroom.
The flow of small talk modifies the architectural encounter.
　　How, Gale thinks, suspecting the glacé cherries of deceit,
How to turn all this once more into a thesis.

　　But there's no Time like the present in the Garden
It begins to hurry the coincidence. It feels strange.
　　Too much Architecture without a helmet,
A disappointed Zara says, all misty-eyed
　　At the latest drawings of the Supplement in Nizam.
Expressively correct and correctly expressive.

Correct it, correct it, the Tarot Readers advise.
Architecture is no longer the eternal promise for that house
     Under the sun. Disappointed? Lord Gale, rumour has it,
Has simulated another Zara and inhabits a
     Virtual Architecture where fiction trails the lights that
Brighten the Ne(x)twork.

     Network, yes, but the errors are attractive.
Sensing a dramatic loss in timing,
     The music hall of Architecture dead on its feet,
The Lobby launches into a repetition of the World's Thinkers
     All beginning with the letter B
Resulting in a repressive lecture on redundancy!

     Whilst in the corner The Flat Tyre ladies
Laugh at others they call the Sparrow-Farters
     And interpret the world's weather
Amongst the chintz and Fatal Air cashew nuts.
     Wonderful to find a new airline so pleased to serve
The Suburbs of the globe with shuttle precision.

     The Flat Tyre ladies complain about redundancy.
They never did like the Cashew Nut service;
     What, after all, has it to do with architecture?
Glory, Glory Allelujah. Glory, Glory Architecture.
     Others sharpshoot at this shaping of a World architecture,
The directive for the future Bill of Fare.

     Walter, the blind architect, enters
White stick tracing the curvilinear handrail.
     Oh God, he says, Architecture's so touching.
But he has no time either. Outside on the piazza
     The One-liners skate out the future city plan
Shifting the city and recolonizing the ghettoes.

The Motor Mouths cut Walter down with a chain saw:
Silence, they announce over the chaos,
    Managing to do all this without resorting to the Panzer tank
On loan from the film crew standing by.
    Silence, again, in three languages.
Architecture, Tourism, and Hotel Management.

    Walter sighs, and has become famous for it.
The blind lead the blind, so much so
    That he has become a bridge across which they trample
All with a duty to invent the theory that will authenticate
    Serious sighing. Short of breath, Walter sits in silence
And invents a conversation with Mr Palomar.

    Oh, Twisters of the World! Oh Integers, Integrate,
Turn lonely chicken wire into displacements of time
    Whilst the space aches to be included in emptiness and
Absence searches for the author to authenticate its inscription.
    Resist, the Gardener says, suddenly indistinguishable
From all those up on the Prize Awards platform.

    No, not likely, Walter says, I do what comes natural.
Apart from ice hockey, I intend to swing by one more
    Time on the way to the Romanesque churches
To get a better look at The Hotel Architecture.
    You drive, I'll talk, Walter says to the Gardener.
Talk, talk, are you kidding? Just drive in silence.

No dark sarcasm in the Lobby of The Hotel Architecture any
    more
No cheap mockery where the Bard embraces the Red Army Choir
And sings
              Why, oh why, Delilah?
History is falsified without us.
Police Chief Delaney still thinks the song should be about him.
Donkeys and Diplomats meet without binoculars
With a hangover and No-return ticket;
Oppositions are no longer oppositions
              But sliders!
Those who wheel on One-liners skating past the Cathedral.
These are the Children of God who know
How the axis of violence has shifted as
Tourism occupies cities losing all claims to their past.

No one has jet lag anymore, you are informed in the passive.
But slouch, they do so, the new Architectural Heroes announce,
Slouch they do towards Dresden or was it Barcelona? The
    Superimposers,
Previously the Weather Forecasters, challenge the Fidgetters
To a game of Ice Hockey. Arrangements are made, up the stairs
                                        On the Mezzanine.
The weather is not wrong but our calenders, Stupid!
Players are bought in, caged. Architects residing elsewhere
Suddenly find themselves living in L.A. or New York City.
Achtung Messieurs et Mesdames, break over, let's nuance this
    statement:
You're not alone, you're never alone!

The parallel visions, temperance, blindess, death and limits
That sort of useful list begins to take over the Tarot Lecture
And Architecture learns to vogue across the ballroom floor.

The Underground Market is all action, where the prostitutes
Lift up their skirts to get the Best Picture of the Year.
Fatal Airlines organises trips to the world's largest cities:
Picture points are guaranteed. Beijing is popular for three days.
One day arriving. One day acclimatising. One day departing.
So quick with the focus and the f-stop. And Architecture?

It's lonely sitting here in deep armchairs
The stale peanuts keep appearing from the seams of the sofas.
It's lonely in the lobby of The Hotel Architecture where,
Cleverer than the conditions we set ourselves,
Architecture struggles to be done straight
                    And yawns more than most other disciplines.

What can we say? Oh Voyagers, Oh Seminal Building
Come to port, this is your real destination.
What more can we give to this condition
But a past and a present with an equal mind?
Some societies do yawn more than others
But those liminal theories come and go;
(*Michelangelo no longer has anything to do with it.*)
Secrets to future buildings are discovered
On long October nights.
Legends follow immediately, uncontrollably.

It's a known fact. The challenge before us all:
To stay awake before the Theatre of Cruelty
Begins where it left off. This time with Motor Saws and
Dump Trucks. Out of the dust on the leather journals come the
Invitations to the world conference on Dittography.
This is no longer ironic for the World is no longer ironic
This is, believe it or not, a genuine invitation.
Never mind that the next century is about to repeat this century;
Nomadism came and went, migrancy with it.
The World is now sitting down again in the Lobby.

Save your coding and body language, another Blind Man says
To anyone who will listen, to anyone without headphones:
Architecture's dead and I'm blind.

Listen up, the Decoders say,
Can't you read between the lines Architecture is offering you?
     High architecture!
     Buy architecture!
And we do, as we prepare for the last tango in The Hotel
  Architecture.
We turn up at the auction, through the restaurant
              To the ballroom and the Awards ceremony
Out on the other side.
When in doubt, the Blind Man says, swerve.
It's the only body language you can pick up in silence.

No, says Uncle Frank, skew with the puck
Before the opponent has time to support the play.

Outside on huge screens,
         The infants who have watched music television
All their life, make movies from what little is left.
It's an elegant exercise in putting to use emptiness.
               Far off
Comes the sound of a Ferrari, a red one seen not long ago
Parked outside the Stone House, purring.
The concrete is all masked, the make-up forever.
No one can find the architect, and the media ask
The publican of the village: Oh yes, certainly some time ago
The Architect passed this way. In a red car? Why yes. In a fast
  car?
Why yes.
A fast car with Laura at his side. The Publican knows more
Than they realise. Laura not Zara? they ask,
Keen to be first with the news of architectural infidelity.

Frank looks around. No sign of the ponytail yet.
Thank god, he thinks
But in a parallel universe, the Blind man says:
I'll be the World's Leading Architect.
Frank leaves. Got to christen the latrines, he says
And swerves. But there's no losing anyone. Everyone is tagged.
The scent of Architecture so strong where the Suburbs
Of the globe have been abbreviated to the Burbs.
Boosterism everywhere. And there's no mistaking this,
The last, very last, tango in The Hotel Architecture.

Hola! In comes El Hombre, out on parole, talking a good game
Motor mouthing on the style of The Hotel Architecture.
A pain in the colon, I'd rather be a dumper than a dumpee.
No one listens. The language is suspect,
A little too much energy in the jaw:
One of those idiolects, picked up in a parallel universe—
Not quite hatched properly.

three **Lullaby Cinema**

Lullaby Cinema, Architecture Sleeps.
When did it become a sickness that we can recall but not explain?
When did all this absurdity become normal, then so inevitable?
And who will announce fatality?

Welcome aboard this Airbus, the Pilot says.

Is that how it's done? Is that how we've written Architecture
Out of our lives, after writing it into our dream?

Saussurisation?
          Pessoa begins polishing the mirror with his own
Breath. Is this all architecture becomes, a character?

Afraid of the telephone, afraid of endlessness, afraid of
Predictability?
So utterly wanting as to be a real pain?
No longer in text but beyond
All timing, pace and action? A strategy to ensure the
Continuity of Solitude? Not the real silence of Architecture
But that irrevocable joy, the beginnings but only the beginnings
Of ecstasy? How many more do we need to teach us the Art of
  Skipping
Yet reading what is forever left to be read and read again for
The First Time? Can we call what we did then Architecture
Any more than what we do now?
                              Who knows besides the Mortuary Attendants,
As they sit out the deaths of others, just what were we doing and
  why.
Whatever it was, of course, it got worse. It is now dying though
We are still unsure what it is dying of. I suspect loneliness.
Old age. And the over-invention of solitude. When I touch the
  hand of Architecture
It is cold. The coldness of a character's hand. The coldness of her
  hand.
And they tell you, you are informed, that you too have it. This
  coldness.
All timing, pace and inaction. All pain.
                    Anatta?

Ah, Architecture with no self. Read: No permanent, singular goal.
Master Eckhart, the pilot, murmurs to whoever will overhear:
The less of self there is, the more there is of self.
That's a funny one but there's no delay, beyond geometry
You must go, beyond all this mental chatter in Architecture. This
  lullaby

Dying down to let the next millennium in? Beyond the beyond the
Meta-grumblers speak about, after Architecture and beyond the
  postmodern mind
Before those trailing have time to catch up. They were told of the
  line but few bothered,
Few had time to read the flow chart before the paperback
  versions

Returned us full circle to those brilliant portraits in convex
  mirrors.
And as if that is not enough, now a song! The Canon, if it has a
  chance, take it
Catch that gleam of light which Emerson tells us flashes across
  the screens
From within, before the lustre of the firmament of beards and
  sages takes over

And padlocks the personal computers. Is it really necessary to
  justify
One's vision of redundancy? Does the Proofreader need
  reassurance?
Does the Underliner need such cheap neon to see through
The alertness of naivety and poke out the innocence of
  Architecture's eye?

The Hoodwinkers, that happy band, those investors in serious
  language,
Anthropologists of a frivolity that lay their boundless scene
  before you
Invite you to become one with the Canon and the World, to
  become one
With the unrest. Can you do it? Come slowly, sing the zero
  summer lullaby

Enter the Garden by the back door, slip the plastic along the
    negative!
Theologically, it slides across the steel channel releasing the
    catch.
A wonderful sound of oil in steel, running better than empty now:
The plate mirroring, the cup runneth over, Architecture sleeps.

four **This Salvaged Mind**

So here I am, in the middle way
Which was one way of putting it. Still not very satisfactory.
You leave the open field a little too hastily,
In your hand a whisky glass from Fatal Airlines.
It's a bit late to begin the uncommitted reading of your own life.
It takes years to journey out of the seriousness
We become to each other. A pity you, too,
Don't read between the lines Architecture is offering you.

Right now, the Car Wash Philosopher says,
It's all about finding a cogito and then we're there, dudes!
Pointing to the One-liners outside on the Cathedral Piazza:
The Final Cogito of Absolute Knowledge!

What? Upset and not convinced, you are invited to push on
And salvage the mind from its savage fate but there's
A crash at reception. El Hombre is trying to exit
But the plastic won't run. The World's on hold anyway.

So what exactly are you implying by your metaphysics?
The Polo Players ask, whilst the anthropologists nod with
    skeletons
Modelled from a delicate birch. Your world is full of postmodern
    knowledge.
How is it used in the postmodern world?

Ditto, Car Wash says, same as last century, same any century,
  Dummy!
That's interesting, the Parachutists say, we've just come upon this:
We know repetition is the answer to all accounting.
Architecture is merely bookkeeping. Shall we say it again?

Let's discuss this on the way to the restaurant,
I'll drive you talk. Or is it the other way round?
Do you mind if I take notes? It's the memory, you see;
After the accident on the podium when the stage collapsed.

Outside the Infants discuss normal dictators with as much relish
As a hamburger dish. The leather book gives off a smell of rose
  water.
Why, no one knows, but it scuffs the writing that will be put
  down in it.
None of your usual lengthy discourse though,

                    (You must remember)
We have been born too late for the spring era,
We lost the reason to understand our knowledge
Many years back. Not meant for this, none of us.
The Garden outside is wounded, bleeding, breaking up. And

There's no novel for the young girl to come through,
To take us back to innocent reading. The dust on the leather
  journals
Is applied. The cocktail shaker is unemployed, aching to correct
  the solutions
That might contain us even more.

Those solutions that should carry the plague dwelling within us.
Architecture indelibly dismembering society. Ah, winningly put,
The Car Wash Philosopher says, it's the bubbles I Iike
As the world watches the huge mops pass over the Ferrari

Like architecure embracing the thighs of women, pretending
   to be
The first feminist discourse. We could go on, maddeningly
   inventive
But irrelevant. Architecture. Fiction. God's speed and others.
None can be quite sure of the regular dosage taken daily.

Obey the dying words? Aphorisms don't bring us more quickly
To a reality resisted through Architecture. Why should we expect
This of language? the Blind Man says on his way back from the
   auction,
Oh and by the way, I just bought the Barcelona Pavilion.

Why should we repeat it? Uncle Frank says, drifting by, I bought
The Villa Savoye! Architecture after all you after *allers* lies outside
Über alles any language used about it. And like me Architecture
Is doubly allergic to the words used to describe its freedom.

Harry, quiet for some time, delivers his thoughts to a tape
   machine.
Architecture, for a period in the future, will be salvaged
To its own soliloquy. It cannot survive the compulsion to
   privatisation;
A salvaged mind is all that's left us. Architecture?

The Parachutists say: Forget it, this is serious. Talent, only skin
   deep.
Genius, forever on the surface. Mediocrity, as deep as ever.
How's that for aphoristic ease? they ask, still using a sponge on
   the window.
Knocking on hell's door. The hell of their own making.

No, Architecture is the blight of interruptions, El Hombre says
As the cashier finally gets his plastic to run with the magnetic.
What were you thinking of before this aphorism? Too late, the
Adjectives thrown around the lobby like soccer balls

Like fine, thin snow, eternal in the harbour wind
Where Columbus points anywhich way. Architecture can't go on
　　like this,
Betrayed building, speaking to each other yet not speaking to
　　each other.
Architectural interpretations, illicitly, forlornly, dropped into
　　faith.

Once again like childhood, blind to all damage.
Tyrannised by such a singular dimension as prejudice.
Such single interruptions that will make Architecture worth more
Than all this language.

Times more remarkable than others, Norton says,
Who finds himself in the Sekunda City in a treacherous epoch
Where times are now more occupied only to be relieved by
　　others.
Why? Why, you ask, unpadlock the computer

When most of us have never ceased giving apologies from birth
To the era, bringing Architecture along
As a welcome interruption, running it
Through our magnetic minds? Still feeling left behind?

five **The Sorceress**

Without appeal you abolish confrontation. The Sorceress enters,
In linen, for the zero summer, and short cowboy boots. Hardly a
　　welcome anymore.
Her scowl tells of the confusion needing reassessment.
She promised the script for World Architecture but with every
　　one
Moved into the editing suite, the intimate histories of humanity
That could have been the guide were ignored. Impatient, the
　　Sorceress

Kicks off her boots and takes a rake to her long buttercup hair.
She's famous for the wide smile
Painted into permanence.
You don't stutter in the garden, you come to a stop.
Ditto Architecture.
                Ditto the Canon.
Today, I have discovered it, the Sorceress says,
Architecture is only useful if it continues to
                        Lose itself to find more.
She crumples the linen into a canvas chair marked Director.
Such a long time since arriving, since space was moved
This century, she cried. If only I'd known then what I know now
I would have handled the Press Conference differently.
I would have known what to say.
Of course, anyone present had the key,
Anyone in The Hotel Architecture could have told her
How to get the creases out with the steam iron.
                        The right temperature
The right imagination allowed to go astray, that sort of thing.
But emptiness begins to see to it gently,
The Sorceress card will be read differently.

Gosh! The Philatelists say:
Why didn't we think of the First Edition, the day and issue
When all the labels pointed to the sky and the bass notes
                Induced the detached gloom of an earth too near?

Surrender now, not likely, but her mind froze, the body dissolved,
Shot so much through with real astrology that when the wind
  began
To ride in me I let the Sorceress go, to become part of the
  Emperor's
Collection of eating utensils and raincoats. Architecture for
  another
World, impregnated against the rain. I took one step up towards

The internal rockery where light fell simulating water and left
The Sorceress to the crumpled linen. Wide awake again
The lucidity of ignorance could have never felt so good
    And fulfilled the Astrologer's promise of a prerequisite joy
        For the next millennium . . .

Resist disturbing the lobby with these insights.
Assume the vision but close the door gently as if you had
Nothing to do with the fireworks being prepared. Do this in
Remembrance of me and remember that the rose bowl really
Doesn't stand a chance and the Third Eye of Architecture blinks
In its own cloud of Unknowing. Only to those who know nothing
  is the secret
So clearly revealed over and over again. And in the redundancy
We have with each other, we find common ground.

The luxuries of multiplicity and plurality are merely entrances.
But once inside, the Sushi Zen master says, it matters not how
You got there, it is a matter of real astrology to stay there.
Steam iron or not, an Architecture to come
        Waiting for new masters.

six **L'Architecture à Venir**

Carmen saw Lord Gale from the hotel window.
I've always loved you, she shouted. Zara, too sharp
For even competition, turned her huge binoculars into a spin.
Shot through the air, they broke Carmen in two.

Zara rises and puts her arms out to greet El Hombre
And for another genetic moment El Hombre
Thinks of the importance of achievement. Too late,
Zara spies the Prize-winner over El Hombre's shoulder.

The Imago Mundi shifts once again on its sword blade.
White Linen, crumpled until the front looks like the back,
Ambles up to Zara; Darling, I didn't think you'd make it.
Emperoratrix, try keeping me away from all this

Deaf poetry of an architectural soul. It's so thrilling, Darling.
But what, except prizes, brings you here
In the foyer of The Hotel Architecture? Zara fingers the
Lapel of White Linen and smooches out the word 'nice'!

There's no time for an answer, Darling, Architecture is now
Following fiction and philosophy. Zara's poetry is well-prepared
Like Total Tennis. Like a shadow the deaf poetry
Starts on the past and undermines that autonomous dusk

That rowdy, drunken laughter that drowns out the stars.
What opinions, Pessoa asks, shall I have tomorrow?
The Foyer doesn't answer, too busy ordering the drinks.
I have no idea, Pessoa answers to the mirror

Since to know that, it would already have to be tomorrow.
Pessoa sizes up Zara and the White Linen suit. Crumpled
An architecture such as this is a perspective devoid of horizon
We fancy. Too many foresee the wrong history and dress up

For the wrong battle. You are all being fooled,
Pessoa keeps addressing himself to the mirror in the foyer
Of The Hotel Architecture. And the worst, if you want to hear,
Pessoa screams until his breath masks the mirror:

You're being fooled without being able to guess the machinery
Of the mechanism which fools you.
Page one hundred and sixty from *The Book of Disquiet.*
I've read it, Zara says, and embraces El Hombre again.

Once, she says, I felt I was part of the Up and Becoming,
But alas, radical otherness has overtaken me.
There, there, don't take it so seriously, Pessoa says,
Everything is after all a degeneration of everything else.

But this cannot be the beginning for Architecture. For there is
    none,
Not even at the end, Zara persists.
The Liminalists in the Lobby limped in, desperate
To explain the sociology of gout. Their bigger

Project was to map The Architecture Genome for themselves.
About this they were keeping quiet until the breakthrough.
The Passport's safe, the Liminalists tell the Foyer, until
Science and Architecture leave you behind. Then start worrying.

Just as the century begins to leave its own architecture behind.
If only you had learnt to leapfrog
Instead of hitchhiking onto the ideas of this century,
Then you'd still be Up and Becoming, they tell Zara.

Unconvinced, Zara turns to the Parachutists. A lively bunch
With silk ties. They always were the ones who entered the
    Garden
Recognising an Architecture outside that familiar framing
Of time and history. They met and exchanged cards in taxis.

No sooner done, they were surfing with some of the century's
    greats.
Paperback stuff, but it didn't matter. Knocking at the window,
This time they learnt from before and inserted
Two stones into the sponge. Turn and turnabout!

And they did. The West, the Parachutists tried to tell us, was
    dissolving
But they too had to wait for the breakthrough before having
The decency to tell anyone. Anyone who stuttered whilst
This was going on gained instant membership to The Hotel
    Architecture.

Anyone who perfected, finessed into a disfiguring event of some
    nerve
Was felt to have, the Committee announced, a certain experience
Of the impossible. Pleased with your detachment in the corner
Of The Hotel Architecture, you seemed to become more famous
    by the Tokyo minute.

The Bucket and Spade card turned up trumps, the Interrogration
    of Rationalism,
As the Futile Paradigm of Language sent out invitations:
Garamond small caps italics, 10 point, elegant with its ambiguous
    claims for universality.
This left the Hasty Renouncers of Dogma somewhat

Amazed at Pessoa, who still talked to the mirror.
What's with the mirror? they asked. You know, don't you,
That it is only an approximation. Some vespers or other
Or some near miss, you mean, Pessoa replied from his own book.

The Hasty Renouncers of Dogma not known for their subtlety
Hastily accepted the few medals that were going (and even a few
Not yet invented). Too hastily, someone noticed the stretching
Of the hairline and began writing out the event for the tain of
    Architecture.

The Lobby in The Hotel Architecture got stranger,
What could they possibly mean? Zara ripped off her dress of fake
    arctic fur
Preferring in the tears and the yarns an Architecture you could not
Possibly hold on to. The gossip had grown since evening.

Now everyone present in the ballroom searched for that elusive
Soundtrack of the century. Lucky enough to enjoy the fiction,
Having resisted a century one has tried so hard to love,
The flared trousers are flaring again, once more catching the
   wind from the side.

Spittoon anthropology dieseled and tortured with an irrelevant
Autobiography which then turn and turnabout resisted
   anthropology.
You will not be invited again, Zara suggests, if you persist
In resisting this deafness of the architectural soul.

A fine mess. But not fine enough apparently. Bull! And Irish too,
The radio tells us to pardon those crossover elements
But exits with the takings for the evening's culture.
The stricter the architect, the stricter the embarrassment,

But the authenticity of jargon suffers,
If you'll once more pardon the awful expression,
From the authentic crossover element. No one listens. Why this
   giving?
Why this taking away? Why this dinner-party embarrassment to
   abandon jargon?

Oh, to establish difference and hijack Architecture's womb.
Really, El Hombre says, were you there? What was it like? Who
   did you meet?
Pessoa wrote up the corpses on the mirror with his breath.
Few had time or cared to read the list.

Those who did, escaped by the first flight out. Fatal Airlines.
They made for Dum Dum Airport. But not before the Thesis was
   out.
Fragmentation took on its own speed. Superficially fragmented,
   the Undecidables
Announce. Apparently fragmented, the Superimpositionists
   interrupt.

Perfectly, imperfectly fragmented, Pessoa says,
But so softly few hear. Rant, El Hombre says, if you say such
  things
Rant, rave, hit the roof. If you want to announce the end of the
  end
Of Architecture, then do it in echo on a sixteen-track machine.

The small water fountain in Dum Dum Airport gives the long
  awaited
Possibility to gulp down the assimilation. Other victims
Gulp empty signifiers and wonder why the cerebral cortex
Registers sadness and melancholy so pleasurably, so deliciously.

The midrift of a woman waiting for Fatal Airlines
Transforms in front of everyone's eyes into a building.
In the electronics shop, the Celebrated World goes on a spree
For the latest global-positioning system for Architecture.

seven **The Parachutists**

We have come to this Hotel to solve Architecture's suicide.
The Celebrated World breathes in double-breasted suits
And it bursts in a drilling of language
Put together into a series of apocalyptic shifts.

Oh Migraine, where are the pills now?
Only now you tell us, if we do not follow
We will never become one of those brilliant unnerring fictions
That Architecture is so good at?

Yet the terrible poetry of violence has to be more than deaf
If we are to get out of here alive and
Go further into the Garden
Than those known attempts at the New Reality.

Don't even think of pausing in The Hotel Architecture Lobby
The Book blurbs are always right
As we relinquish the models of instant myth
Like hydrogen-filled balloons brought to a cemetery.

The Parachutists look on thinking of beginning their own
    movement.
If only, they say to themselves, the Architect
Could have come up with the shape of a whale
It would swim there, into view, for all to see.

How could I refuse its being? How could I refuse its logic?
The Car Wash Philosopher interrupts the Architect.
The Parachutists reply angrily, We do wish you'd wash and go!
Delivered with a little more vehemence than normal.

But it's obvious, as we leave the Lobby of The Hotel
Architecture and enter the Millennial Lounge:
Ideology is on the edge of another nervous breakdown.
The helicopter will not land

The camera pans as the rape continues, just *out of site*.
In the lounge money is still the model of life unwanted
Still out of their skin and overdetermined,
Predisposed factors land in paper aeroplanes

Sent from the back seats by the Reserve Crew.
The Parachutists begin deconstructing the figures;
The Superstructure, Ah, the superstructure, they nod
With a generous wink at Laurence Sterne and Jean Luc Godard.

But the Reserve Crew didn't get it, missed the B-team altogether.
They stopped getting the world's jokes some decades back.
I don't understand your question. We don't understand
What you are doing here. And why we are here . . .

Unless it is to extract the grenade pin. Oh Burnt Norton!
What Little Bidding is given your dwelling on this earth?
There are some in the Hotel who have got in without tickets.
The Unreconcilables begin to itch in their undersized suits

Their footwear disappoints, nothing svelt
Too much scuffing along the Academy corridors
In search of that nonformal rationality.
The skaters have accelerated into the fast lane

They score by the minute and drag Architecture with them
Turning the Cathedral Piazza into an arena.
The Dog trainers have their hoops out and watch
The Architects jump flames into Grenade City.

Someone (*who could it be?*) hooks up with the city's speakers
And we hear an invitation, more an appeal, to the ball:
We must organise the unorganisable.
We must reconcile the irreconcilable.

We must dissociate the dissociable. It drones on.
Quickly they rush to the Parachutists. Confusingly
They rename themselves the Superimpositionists;
A gentle gang if ever there was one

Playing with notions that will put dust back on the rose bowls,
Death back in the Garden. And hydrogen in the balloon.

eight **Little Bidding**

Midwinter spring in the Hotel is its own season.
Even the One-liners learn to apply their knowledge
Like swapping ice-hockey cards from chewing-gum packets.
Instead of jostling, bouncing it off the walls, any three walls

They are learning to return it worse for wear.
The local radio station, The Colon, invents the news
Requested that morning. The soul's spa still quivers.
Spoken with pain, it awaits the arrival of something profound.

That is something profound to substitute for the last profundity.
Oh where is the summer, the unfilmable zero summer?
Memos for the next millennium are turned out by the lorry load
But the applause is not deafening, it is orchestrated.

And when it arrives, if it came this way, taking any route,
Starting from anywhere, at any time or any season,
This profundity is pounced on. Very wise, the Disk Jockey says,
If you also remember ash on the living legend's sleeve,

And communication tongued with fire and mixed with the red
    wine,
Flavouring the camembert the Legend loved so much.
                        Wisdom passes this way
At the intersection of that timeless moment. We saw it coming,
It failed to check in at The Hotel Architecture, but no one can
    deny it.

The baton was dropped. Only those who fudged this century
    wanted to film it.
The others balled the wall and got out whilst there was still time
Bouncing themselves off three walls in a velcro game:
Architecture told how to return without passing Go!

Being dead as the Parachutists eat the pasta, drink the melange
And polish their ceramic floors, the Car Wash Philosopher,
Haircut by appointment only, gives more fundamental reasons
Why he should be fundamentally ignored.

A lifetime passes. The turbo car comes and goes, no substitute for
   the Ferrari
But more friendly on the lightweight travel suit and palmtop
   computer.
Nothing left but to check out of The Hotel Architecture
Anytime you like, anytime of year.

The willful logic of the Up and Becoming continually—never and
Always—missing the point of their own talent. Once more
At the intersection, they start looking like termites
On the attack. We were there before you, the termites say,

Before your exhibitions. Cleverer than our words yes, but
Not our deeds. But the tidy radicalism and slow erotics
Pass for something close to contemporaneity.
But I guess they know they are being talked about

And wonder, as they mount the steps, how to avoid that
Possible trip on the route to the Awards Podium.
Being talked about makes all the difference. Sadly, being explicit
Isn't the crime it was. It is the language of the living.

nine **Wretched Unscience**

No one visits the Living Legend anymore. He sits with the
Mortuary Attendant present. Still, of course, addressed as *Maestro*.
But no one arrives to the private suite in The Hotel Architecture.
Out of bounds, no one risks a visit whilst the stakes are so high.

He walks up there in the private suite, activities continuing down
  in the lobby.
A film of his own life shows over as Architecture mourns more
  solitude
And the shuffling characters of the world's carnival dream whilst
For the untalented, a wretched unscience undoes the world
  achieved.

When there were conversations, long ago, names are now
  unrecalled.
Only the slow shuffling walk and the mumbling remain clear. It is a
Desperate move. The Archivists falter as they try and make the
  Legend live
What he hasn't, what he didn't. This, our Last Architectural Hero,
                     Forbids feeding as much as Architecture.

No real existential consolation anymore, he says. The Mortuary
  Attendant
Sees no real cause for alarm. Nothing extraordinary
                 In the worsening situation;
Always an explanation ready for future pain. Life, the Attendant says,
Has always been a translated sentence. The studio

Always a room full of paper when it wasn't corpses, the *machine-
  à-écrire*,
A boat and an open sea. How did it happen? That he could die
  walking,
Like Architecture? The Attendant warns that speech is lessening.
One day it does not get up. Architecture dies, still being filmed.

What was that period and how did it begin? Architecture was
  explored.
It was tongued but nothing was in its speech. As words die on us,
  the idea of anything
Closer to him than Architecture was a forbidden thought.
L'impossible! Anything like love could not get closer.
              It was forced to take a taxi

To the small studio at the top of The Hotel Architecture. And
   we've seen
All the films twice over. Visits were minimised.
Architecture had to reinvent solitude to survive the
Wretched Unscience he dreamed about for so long. After
   Architecture

No aphorisms saved him, no popular song lifted him.
He served tea but drank it himself whilst Architecture became
   background.
Two or three musical pieces could be heard from the stairwell
Of The Hotel Architecture. All playing simultaneously.

Achieved, then, no foreground existed for Architecture.
                          He wanted to be further in,
Or then move further on than any architecture could take him.
After the film of the book, after Architecture done straight
Once more, it was too late. He knew he was dead. He could feel it.

ten **The Science of the Singular**

Rise, put poetry into the philosophy it will never become
Put Architecture into the public fear of its own future.
The Superimpositionists practise announcing themselves:
They rehearse their entrance, occupying the grand paradox
With scarcely a different credit card. Laminates, they scoff!
Merely Global Positioning Systems they carry around with them;
But without the ocean, they read only how we cannot proceed.
A gentle Repetition. No Bucket and Spade for this.
The Superimpositionists play ball. The cricket sweaters have a
   green
And violet V-neck. Trimmed. The knee pads will take their fall
   in language
The T-shirt slogans will invent another *biodata* for Architecture's
   corpse.

We must proceed, we can't proceed. We will Proceed!
Having heard it before doesn't matter. Architecture takes us
Into the Millennial Ballroom where a dome is planned;
Architecture now has a thesis but misses the story.
In a monotone the world takes shape again and misses the
Point of its talent. Speech is slurred, then recorded.
Architecture is dyslectic, a stranger to its own theories.
The Authenticity of jargon needs the trigger to invert itself into
                                   The Jargon of Authenticity
Only then, the Superimpositionists say, is it possible
To go for the haircut.

What? the Barber says. A plain card this:
Christophe or Philippe. Haircuts by Appointment at Railways
    Stations
Or Air Terminals. There but for the trimming, go I.
Dislocating and then swerving from the scalp
In another way to end the topos of heterogeneity.
Gel? Christophe interrupts.

The Topos of Heterogeneity! That's what I said,
The Superimpositionist tries to get in on the act
Whilst Christophe massages the architectural skull as if
Rehearsing a sherry trifle.

One of those Irreconcilables breaks in.
What now? Isn't this the next millennium already?
Why all this cake and eat it undecidability?
Why can't we slip into a supplement of difference
Become *artificiel* and take up the rhetoric of labour itself?

Outside the Infants have taken over.
They redefine collage
Like the quicker skaters who race with the dogs
The blood out on the cathedral piazza now dry.
That which does not exist,
Calls us slowly from the Ballroom to the Garden,

Rose petals now on the plate under the warming lamp
Tanning nature. Architecture asks, pleads, begs to become
More than an event of itself where traipsing
Room after room gives way to a sequence.
Finally in the lobby we recall, one and all,
Our anthologies under our arms: You can exit anytime you like
But you can never leave The Hotel Architecture.
You need only light up *le cricket* that belongs to the B-team
To find the coffin lid well and truly shut.
Only a little gas left, then out with this Architecture.
But who believes in it?
There's no one left to explain it
And no reason for anyone to do so.
The building is now a labyrinth to itself;
Digital-entry controls have the advantage of turning around
The Hotel so that each morning, unaware of the tilting world
The Superimpositionists and the Parachutists
Set out from entirely different points of departure.

Each morning, they begin again in a different Hotel
With time getting a little nearer the Press Conference and
The Awards Ceremony. No one gets there but the promise
  remains.
Each morning, all architects returning to Go
Without passing the swimming pool!
. . . .
Oh *Fortuna!* World Architecture
Wondrously freed from its wishfulfilled legacy.
It is me that stutters now, sponge dipped in neon,
                  Two pebbles turn and turnabout
Knocking on the window, trying to find my way
                  In order to stay lost.

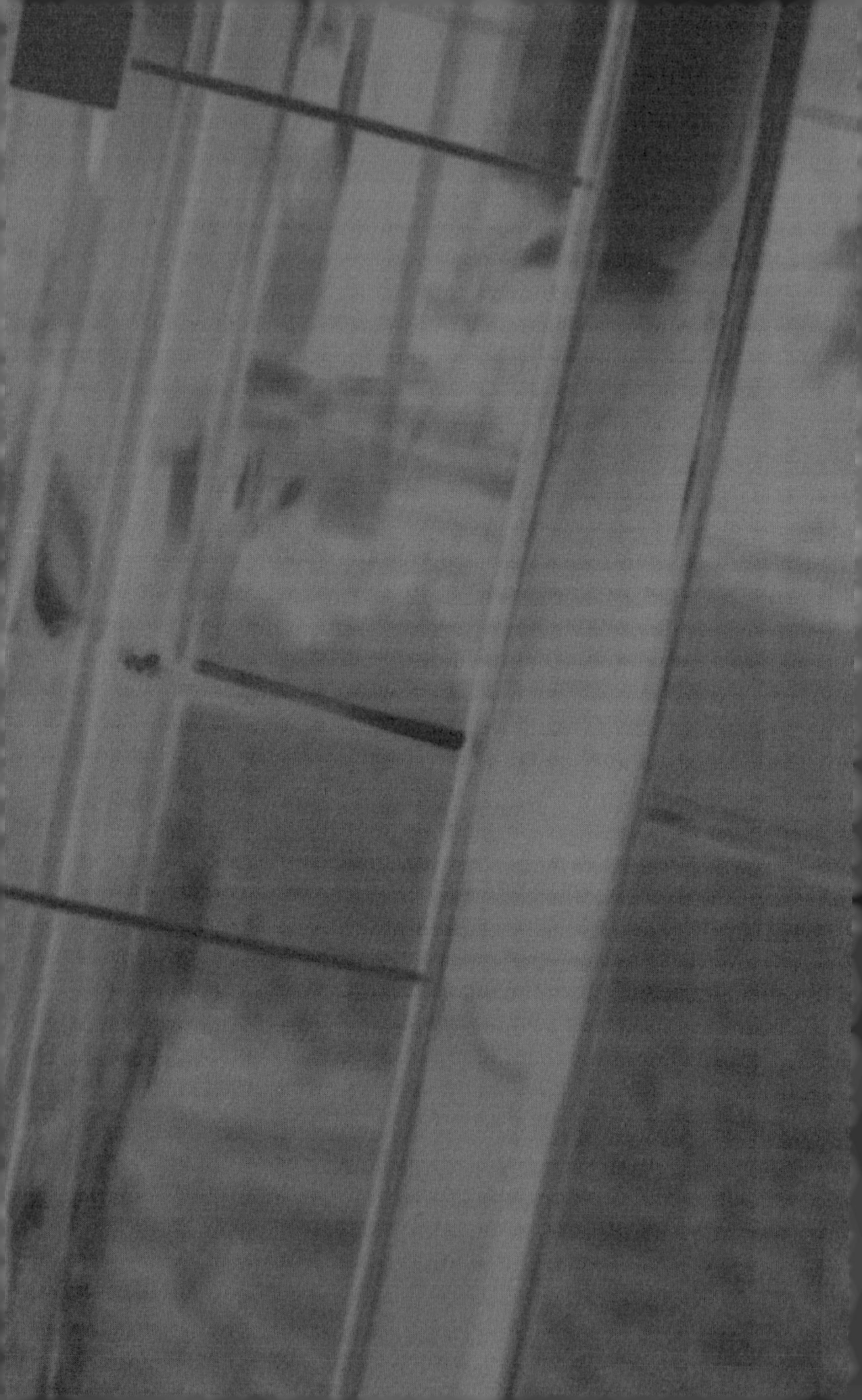

Part Four **Ditto! Architecture**

May your shadow never grow back
May it always leave you behind

one **The Virtual Seminar**
(Going Beyond the Seas)

I hear that the axe has morphed,
Paul Antschel says ahead of all of us
Changing the name to suit the city lost.

I hear that the place can't be named
But if you do attempt the television series
Then remember the dangerous shadows.

I hear that the bread which looks at him,
(*Paul logs into his own poem*) Heals the hanged man,
And is baked for him by his wife.

I hear what you call our only refuge, Architecture
In this digital lounge has for us
Become a wease.

I hear the machines have moved in
Console stations set up everywhere,
Conduits laid, satellites paid.

I hear the Digital City is already upon us,
No change of address this, just a tease!
It is not *We* who are leaving.

I hear the overpriced software
No longer outrageously named Auschwitz
Means all poems like Architecture can be saved

Called up on screen, altered, waved:
Architecture via French philosophy famed,
On its return journey, coming back to us.

But it is not *We* who are doing the sighing.
No longer this intolerable heaviness
Lowered regularly on the hour's squeeze.

It is another Welcome quite apart
To the digital lounge right in the heart:
Anytime you like, Any screen you please

At The Hotel Architecture
Such a lovely place, such a lovely space
Any time of day . . .

You can check out any time you like
But you can never leave
A convenient line Architecture has us so believe

A paradox, too, for the fisher of pike.
But all this lowlying wisdom, lets the Era grieve
For it's a sonnet, right now, we are supposed to conceive

So let's try it out before we *The Wretched* lose all control
Bringing down on us the wrath
Of Modernism's most famous rose bowl.

two **Sonnet Boom!**

DITTO! large were the words carefully scrawled
On the newly configured electronic mail box.
So to rid this discipline of its low accursed pox
To a mission higher, we are now supposedly called,
Before we find ourselves so philosophically mawled
By another rhyme without adequate reason
Residing in The Hotel Architecture off off-season
Realising a superstructure, limpid, so appalled.

We beg to reintroduce Architecture's wit and charm.
But a Neo-poetics of Space, not quite that, No!
Otherwise may we not inadvertently do more harm?
Instead something light, allowing us all to grow
    An intelligent Archetypal then, embracing chance
    Or an Architecture soaring, Asterisque's dance?

three **Phew!**

Phew, Archetypal and Asterisque
Two characters indeed worth the wait
Finding themselves on the hard disk
Surely no one can now say it's too late.

Forget, they plead, the longish introduction,
The unrhymed reason of architectural space,
Go for the absent present, the tele-symposium
The looser, juicier gossip of race.

Service teams begin, screen-wise, to hover low
Seemly, the slightest glitch meanly unfurled
Testily waiting to hear their own lonely echo
Cyberspace: ditto ditto the word's world.

After all, were not each of us told
On a return trip stopover cocktail JFK,
No one need move from, let alone hold
To such devastatingly lonely architectural play?

Ditto. Ditto. Phew Ditto thrice
The same events recur more than twice
Back and forth go couplets in rhyme
Let's agree with Beckett, it passes the time.

If that was or was not the sonnet it should be
An Ode to Architectural Repression we'll have to free
And leave the last two lines in questions afloat
Constraint, foreclose it, but don't ever gloat.

Should Architecture then be mildly unique
A trim slim excellence with mediocre longing?
Or enwombed in this literary hide-and-seek
Autographs only, media audience thronging?

Nothing outside The Hotel Architecture!
Can Jacques the Fractalist be this forgiven?
La Folie, that lived-in French prefecture
Bemused, besmitten, besmirched, bestriven.

This fragmenting experience should it not be all
Our tame imaginations so delicately require?
Soft passions for simultaneity rise and fall
As the Skate-of-the-Art Boarders take us higher.

Outside the Hotel, the Roller Bladers get more daring
Single lines weave electric through the screen
And Digital Bliss begins to have another bearing
On those far-off agendas, sight sited so unseen.

If this is Architecture then I'm less than alive,
The Silver Knight returned from Hong Kong says.
From his Thames seat old cars he espies, in his drive;
Build brighter, chrome up Guys! Change your ways

And let's have no more of this Gossip, light and inane
No more unrest, nor shall philosophy ever enter here.
My son's not called Jack and my mirror has no tain
Got it! Architecture but one millennial agenda to clear.

four **The Architect to the Philosopher**
(On a Discipline Fast Fading)

Architect
We will not cease the Poetics or Gossip of Unrest
Until Architecture itself has become
The gossip of eternity blessed.

Philosopher
This was how it started. Preventing foreclosure's urge,
Warnings against taking the sense of sense
Too seriously, began an unstoppable purge.

Architect
A touch rough alright, but let the editorials plead
Though suffering from immediacy's sin
Despair becomes millennial greed.

Philosopher
You cannot hold us to blame, it really is a scam
Neither are we to blame when your Text
Turned out to be a sham.

Architect
Cunningly, you slip us out of our own texts with wit
Into something comfortably disrobed;
Until indecision enters, dryly illicit!

Philosopher
Frankly no one cared that there was nothing anymore
Outside the text: the artful slogan
Which stripped you all numb to the core.

Architect
Like the Hotel, you mean, always checking out
    Of language whenever we liked;
        Aphasic discipline in the middle of a rout.

Philosopher
Archetypical of you to lay the blame here
    When the shopping spree was over and done.
        Moderation always was your discipline's fear.

Architect
Yes, certainly, on that you cannot be faulted
    We never did get the satisfaction
        The songs claimed. We were sorely assaulted.

Philosopher
Deprived, I'd say, of course whiter than white
    Your buildings with the economy pack
        Turned into finessed disasters overnight.

Architect
Oh and I suppose you'll rub it in and go on to say:
    Blurred the angled agony of displacement
        And our taste for fashion on the way.

Philosopher
Taste, after a fashion, always your discipline has sought.
    I couldn't have put it better. You yourselves
        Reduced the headlines to architectural sport.

Architect
Told not to go for the quick-fix solution,
    No time to go into detail. Is it our fault
        Discourse turned into seductive pollution?

Philosopher
Reduced to the eternity of your gossip. Fatal!
Just what did you honestly expect
Out of ideas so restless, so prenatal?

Architect
True, we all got carried away on the world tours.
Vying with each other to invent such lines:
My propaganda machine is bigger than yours!

Philosopher
You suffer for it, the rumours are out on Easy Street.
You, wedged now in the Museum of Disasters
Alongside brothels, Porsche ads, infected meat.

Architect
Oh, it's fine for you to sit there, smoke, and gloat;
The thinness of all Theory and Reason
Blame it all on us, yes, you stubborn goat!

Philosopher
Steady on there, you invited us into this dump.
You it was who announced the end of the Sick Parrot Era.
You were the ones begging 'style' to jump.

Architect
Oh, so now Philosopher, the Era of the Cuddly Toy?
Decoded, disrobed, forgive us all.
Slip on the CD, Beethoven's *Ode to Joy*.

Philosopher
Oh Architect! Don't forever meta-grumble.
Beware the Hoodwinkers in your midst;
Can't you see, it's you and you alone they humble.

Architect

Thanks for the advice, though why right now
As thinness has for so long stood in
Should we to philosophy scrape and bow?

Philosopher

Don't tell me, really, it comes as such surprise;
The Academy Leaders have slyly encouraged you
To forget essential architectural alibis.

Architect

So, we've been royally, absolutely, academically duped?
Is there no real hope nay chance,
Has the Century's narrative so coolly looped?

Philosopher

Little patience left for your type of strip poker.
The screens ultimately blur, fail and spin,
Leaving you, Architect, the eternal joker.

Architect

You mean, in the pack there's nothing to offer, no more
The capacity to pass from one life
To another. Meaning: no score draw?

Philosopher

Not even, that is, to die in only one life's breath.
Everything even Auschwitz tells you,
You don't ever quite beat death.

Architect

So what is it now you suggest Philosopher, pray!
Leave indecision forlorn, foreclosed
For just one more zero summer day?

Philosopher

Oh Architect, don't attempt so weakly this poor science
Of hijacking hermeticism. Without
Acknowledging our forewarned alliance.

Architect

Death, you mean, to language, Architecture, and scale.
Score more points, forget it quick,
Roll the dice or Go to jail?

Philosopher

Ditto Architecture, now you're talking.
To beat Architecture's slow decline
Keep walking, walking, walking.

Architect

Right into philosophy, the activity of the night
Installed for eternity's answer.
Stutter, then, until we get the line right?

Philosopher

Ah Architect, I think you've learnt bit by bit
An Architecture never quite so unsimple
You need score more points than it.

five **Jack's Kitchen**
(Any Husband to Any Wife)

So where, when the next Discourse
Tropes into existence, perforce

Will you be? Down Columbus Avenue
Left by the shops, avoiding the queue

Past the gaping cashpoint
Past the hot Annapurna joint

Abandoned cadillac, torn steering wheel
The days of chaos and riot, state unreal.

Further on over from Brooklyn
Some way off the Holiday Inn

Lightness (*the darkness of*) tilts the Axis Mundi.
Whilst PC graduates discuss (*the lamentable*) Burundi.

The factions split asunder
No 'Afrifuckinwonder'!

Whilst the coolest dudes
Those way ahead, not all pseuds

Drag the unprejudiced cursor along
Humming the Fisher King's naked song

Over Base Camp Icon Central Park
Past Dakota's unforgiving dark.

Memory returns to haunt the screen
       As thereupon the mouse
Downloads an immaculately restored
       Elizabethan manor house.

An eternal return to the first world
       Emerges, a gentle slide
To Baldwin Manor in the 'real'
       Cambridgeshire countryside.

The home of Jack Wagstaff,
      Professor of Dittography.
The long-awaited newest chair,
      Hottest after Geo-chronology.

After first making its delicate way
      Across the paper clips and weights,
The camera establishes the 'mental map',
      Geography's enticing silver gates

From which we are all supposed
      To leave with joy and glee.
To encounter the other worlds
      Advertised by anthropology.

Clever, will architects soon become,
      To control and shift the undrawable
Into an Architecture all their own,
      So slyly wily laudable.

All but forgetting the decades,
      The centuries, the darker years
In a bid to make the architectural bull
      From Mickey Mouse's ears.

The meal, silently being prepared
      In Jack's kitchen: game.
Drinks are silver-served, of
      Gestalt and Tectonics fame.

Invitations for a rival symposium
      On Dittography ready
Laser printed, folded, enveloped:
      Not a hand unsteady.

In case the electronic mail
    Loses its willing backer
To an outrageously discontinuous,
    Nonlinear *gaia* hacker.

The cat, Sam, named after Johnson
    Decides to bring in a bird.
Plucked from the cat's mouth,
    Immediately an absurd

Exercise in rewriting the sequel.
    No, not another Hotel
This should be more accessible,
    Preferably a dusty motel

Fast-forwarded to Tijuana
    Hotel Americana Twenty-third.
And what should we find
    But a wounded tasty bird

High up there on the ledge
    Permanently sealed
Precarious game unreachable
    Solution revealed.

We have been told before
    But so few keep track.
It's worth keeping up, they say,
    Otherwise you'll be back

To where you started.
    Architecture's undoing,
A writing askew that can never quite
    Match this guileful wooing.

But it's a run for the money and
          No one really avoids
The swimming pool temptation after
          All the crashes at (London's) Lloyd's.

So World Architects envy Jack
          The higher form of life.
A long day off with G & T
          Any husband to any wife.

And Jack in one of his delightful
          Postprandial games
Gives to this contest, Gestalt
          And Tectonics, their names.

A literary gest, of course,
          More at home in brutalist Churchill,
Ushers in a whole series of tactics
          For which known Researchers will kill.

Also for a Higher Architecture
          Superior in language found.
A battle with opponents
          G & T Unbound.

Literature, philosophy, civilisation:
          And culture sticks again.
Isolated from its modern calling
          Architecture feeling the pain

It lodges there in the throat
          Like pitted orange-peel.
Lobbied, unsettled relentlessly
          Thick-cut, reformist zeal.

Privatisation of all things closest
    Is ambiguously recommended
If Architecture is still up
    To be challenged, extended.

Jack exits, promising next time
    To explore rabbit cuisine,
But is now distracted with one such
    One touch, electronic queen

Picked up in Cambridge, software-ready,
    Auschwitz-clone;
The condition of knowledge
    In the ambivalent zone.

The 'liminal paradigm' unzips itself
    An all-embracing feat.
Theory and practice of translation
    The menu's exemplary suite

Between the objective world of experience
    And the constructed
Subject, centripetal and centrifugal
    Timelessness inducted.

Architecture joining and separating.
    Oh Fortuna abandon
The very migraine the next century
    Already has a hand on.

six **Oh Fortuna**

Oh *Uticitas!*
No dust settling on this rose bowl
No corridors down which . . .
No conversation allowed that . . .
Nothing to alter the already achieved but . . .
No option but for Architecture to reappear as . . .
A character in its own narrative
        As system and structure.

Oh *Venustas!*
Tempting us into a redundancy with . . .
With all the machinations of . . .
Against which the lizards try on . . .
Tight, very tight Italian shoes as . . .
A substitute for their very own
        Cultural and symbolic frame.

Oh *Fortitas!*
Retrieving themselves in the vocabulary like . . .
Actors investing Godot with their own . . .
Order, meaning, and values such as . . .
A silk bicycle balaclava,
That hat trick which . . .
Passes the time that was there
        But to pass itself away.

Oh *Rosencrantz!*
Borrowed from the fringe when . . .
Time would have passed anyway anywhere . . .
Limning all the promising architects who . . .
Find their favourite non-place whilst . . .
Hiding the actors in barrels of tar and . . .

Dis-figuring them as only words do
                    To the unknown faces.

Oh *Guildenstern*!
Where mental chatter and experience is . . .
Not only communicated and reproduced but . . .
Transformed, a new lease of death and . . .
A redundant project, of course . . .
Leaving happily what Architecture
                    Leaves happily unthought.

Oh, *Philosopher!*
If, as you claim . . .
The future lies in . . .
The suburbs of the globe then . . .
The future of this future lies . . .
In the suburbs of the suburbs
                    Of the Universe next door.

Oh *Architect!*
Always travelling never arriving . . .
Stop to every arrival everywhere and . . .
No longer following all this . . .
Responding to a condition which . . .
Is increasingly shaped by forces
                    Beyond Architecture itself.

Oh *Frank!*
Are you still here so brave . . .
Haven't you given up . . .
Excited and exited . . .
Out of here after installing . . .
Over seventy computers in the office after . . .
Providing a master switch
                    And padlocking the mouse.

Oh *Harry!*
You, too, still walking across . . .
Paris, Texas plain as . . .
Such was the stuttering towards . . .
The Vocabulary of the marketplace and . . .
Architecture where language chronicled lay
                    In that hotel room where . . .

Oh *Resenter!*
You get the gist of . . .
The Milennium where . . .
The authenticity of . . .
Jargon did . . .
Give way momentarily
                    To the jargon of authenticity.

Oh *Director!*
The film paused at . . .
We all paused at . . .
The system was down so . . .
The ballroom ceiling ripped out because . . .
The angles tilt, the slabettes arch
                    In agony and overlay.

Oh *Asterisque!*
Language easier than it was . . .
The integers unsteady for . . .
As the sensuality of . . .
Rocked planes keep . . .
Crashing through the interior
                    Of The Hotel Architecture.

Oh *Archetypal!*
The Illusion of order so . . .

Discursive upheaval of . . .
Spiral of tensions like . . .
A spitfire entering the lonely restaurant
                    Of Planet Architecture.

Oh *B-team!*
You with the Bucket and Spade . . .
You arriving early . . .
You *bricoleurs* who . . .
With a wisdom unbowed . . .
Stutter . . .
Caress yourselves into the final poem
                    In the tarot sequence.

Oh *St. Perec!*
Death and a return to Go . . .
Without passing the swimming pool . . .
Anyway, Anytime, Anywhere . . .
Architecture, a User's Manual . . .
Arm in arm with the victims
                    Rounds up the usual suspects.

Oh *Bataille!*
The greatest intellect . . .
Written in . . .
Against Architecture . . .
The Impossible Manual where . . .
Architecture is always
                    The most easily duped.

Oh *Survivor!*
You think you read and . . .
Survive the lines . . .
Lonely in your own . . .

Alphabet of distress.
You . . .
You succumb to the fetishism
            Of Architecture's own recluse.

Oh *Morris Minor!*
The Hotel Architecture cannot but . . .
Choose particular words in order . . .
To de-light in them . . .
With the lightness of . . .
The malaise of the perverse
            Puns from Paris.

Oh *Pont Neuf!*
That in Paris . . .
Always assumed a . . .
Straight, if hidden usage . . .
Where . . .

Oh *Planet Architecture!*
If you could empty yourself of . . .
If you could embrace the rumbling in . . .
If you can navigate the lizards there . . .
If you can leave scarce friendship behind . . .
You might . . .
Witness the beginning
            Of a beautiful relationship.

Oh *Beastly Poem!*
Beyond itself . . . beyond geometry
Beyond architecture . . .
Beyond distress flares . . .
Beyond impasse . . .
Beyond language . . .

Beyond autobiographical error
         And fatal attraction.

Oh *Polish idiom!*
Stumbled upon . . .
Long after the cat . . .
Has been caressed to death . . .
Long after returning to Go . . .
Without forfeit . . .
Welcome to The Hotel Architecture
         Where clarity begins at home.

seven **Digital Lounge Lizards**

Digital lounge lizards at work in the wingchairs
Music playing continuously, up go the distress flares

Electronic notebook, malt whisky, crystal glassware,
Books, rare, used, paperback. All ditto, past care.

Scales up, lizard-fresh, out of the Academy run
Two of the bald Masters seeking architectonic fun.

Fighting over the use of the Designer comb
Race you there and back, they say, and then home!

Fond are they of overstating metaphysical reach.
Gestalt versus Tectonics, Powerbook on the beach.

Gin versus the tonic, no time to document it.
Approximation refined takes them to the limit.

Whilst rudeness with instinct redesigns reality
Fills the Smart Bars with a vital brutality.

DITTO badges are everywhere, thrillingly disloyal
Bids to communicate the epoch. Just a shaky foil.

For the new behaviour guidelines circulated as fast
As they can be reworded to outdo, outplay the past.

It isn't about space, the Master of Ceremonies says.
It's about desire, convention, statics: Life's dull replays.

They've always been a scaffold for the lonely metaphors
Necessary for a private life to interrogate its cause.

The logic is flawed, the Smart Bars know it.
Architecture remains tagged, ever more likely to blow it

On the electronically ransomed, the nonlinear Dream
As long as we ourselves remain discontinuously seen.

The French publisher rushes into the Lobby
I'm tempted to say with his playmate Bobby

Running his fingers too across his bald pate
For the fight over the comb a fraction too late.

Watches material made Image, Historicism edged out.
Barely can he contain his desire to shout.

Inside out of the drench, for it has begun to rain
As this was originally all set in a fictional Spain.

The publisher delighted, the work is not out of reach
Of the new *Cyclopaedia*, he thinks will ultimately teach

All those who think Architecture has become such a bore
Something flaky, dull, mythic, little more than folklore.

Nostalgia for the future is gaining ground, he faxes back
To someone in Paris. Secretary? Amanuensis? No, hack!

Architecture made real by realising such easy lines
Once again just a matter of rereading the old signs.

Advertise! The Publisher considers this a major factor
Avoiding those lizards searching for the strange attractor.

This is the future, the Publisher states. We must be there
Whatever it takes. Armani, silk ties, mega-hold gel in the hair

Grey beard, double chin, bloated stomach. Architecture, nothing
   like pity.
The era of mountain bikes is back: Revenge on the city!

eight **Hiroshima Software**
(The Worlde a-Hunting Is . . .)

Changing down a gear or two
Brevity is now the precious clue.

Architecture. *C'est drôle!*
On this, the digital roll.

Fiction of the epoch, good good wine
Shaky shaky shaky! Nineteen-sixty-nine

The French Publisher replies,
I've been here before. He lies

I have cruised the watchtower,
Seen the Situationists cower

Drift and rise from out of Althusser's death
The Manual on Everyday Modern Breath.

Have passion for this little neon louse.
And for usage I, too, can move a mouse

For the principle neat tectonic scheme
For years has been my secret dream.

And lightness from this darkened screen
Will always offer more for Architecture's scene.

So, cut and paste as much as you like,
But Hype and Hooch never spike.

For further details drag the cursor,
Stuff the mouse. It can be no terser.

Roll the ball, the lizards do it so fast.
To the Second World before it too is past

After Auschwitz redefined space and law,
Architecture after the Second World War.

Dumb snow? Stalingrad and Hiroshima
The Directors couldn't have been much keener.

Erase! Couldn't get there fast enough!
Each from his wing chair shouts: Tough!

On the Highway so unsafe; terminal slump.
The Near-famous Architects delicately dump

Their oscillating deployment of form and scale.
As excavations of the future they are often pale

Leaving others to make the jargon fit its use
Hunting and applying ideas more or less obtuse.

The highway drifts, from Treasure Island nightly
To where Architecture performs ever so tightly

To Lapland where the ornamental poet for fun
Writes messages on the screen in Sami to his son.

Be home, when I get there, see you Dad!
In an Arctic minute! That's my lad.

It's digital time way up there in cosmic Lapland
Where the vast snow seems so tantalisingly grand.

A gentle Architecture of unrest unwinds certainly
Car boots, velcro, trailers and tree tree tree.

Hiace trucks, traffic bollards and bailing twine
Planking, straw bails plus the odd Elk sign.

Spruce branches, circus tents, polythene and bars
And a majestic farting parade of old American cars

Repressed, economic, picturesque if not exactly mosaic
Tectonics minus gestalt, somewhat dangerously archaic.

Yet for new visions of The Hotel Architecture's Room
We suggest you refer back to the sonnet in Sonnet Boom

As we now know Virtual Reality surely means,
Representation beyond all these cinema screens.

There's no time left, no garden, no foil, no door
No dumb snow to spin this out any more.

Jargon gets but one, and one chance only
Before inauthenticity, sad and lonely

Out on the cynical highway, ceases killing us
And Architecture the enigma keeps on billing us.

The waiters arrive with what little movements left.
The words they have avoided—intelligent, deft—

Get less and less, as their importance rises
Until the Chairman blows the whistle: No more surprises . . .

At this symposium, please. It is Repetition Day
Our sort of Architecture always liked it that way.

nine **All Along the Highway**
(*Unplugged*)

There must be some kind of way out of here,
Said the Lone Ranger to the Dean
This is only confusion about confusion
I'm really no longer that keen

Highway punks, they drink our wine
And Microserfs dig our earth
None of them along the line
Know what any of it is worth

(*anymore*)

No reason to get dispirited,
The Dean he kindly spoke
There's many here in Architecture
Who feel the Highway but a joke

And you and I, we've been through this,
And this is not our future
So let us not talk jargon nor
Architecture long passed 'suture'

All along the Highway
Millennium kept in view
While Lightness came and went
Obfuscations too

Outside in the distance
A Wild Card did growl
Two subtexts were approaching
The Net began to howl.

ten **Song of Whatever (sic)**

We never meant to be rude,
Nor even actually to be that crude
But there are so many out there
Who honest, just don't really care
Don't give a damn, certainly not a monkey
To them Architecture's lost, not even funky.
So perhaps it's right, was right all along
To plunge right here into the *whatever* song.
For more pressing concerns like the IRA
The Michael Collins' story, war and play
Leave us wrong to think it finished there
Virtually passing Go, to arrive with no flair
Under the dinner table to prattle and scupper
At the Near-famous Architects' last supper.
So it's best to come clean and simply serve
The readers who think unkindly we've lost nerve.
Somewhere in Central Europe, out came a thriller.

From the deeper shadows of Goethe and Schiller,
The bright idea of a Crisis Line was born
Digitally linked, cables under the lawn
On into the lungs, right into the tomb
Of The Hotel Architecture's Cabinet Room.
The lizards were jumping, this was something new
Ditto! Eat the heat, no one had a clue.

A new direction this was, the Culture of Complaint
Architecture's Life-on-Line served by a Crisis Saint.
Advice was available, you simply just had to call
Confess, talk of Whatever, its rise and fall
How language has moaned, twisted and turned
Until no option left but to be rejected, spurned
By the unguarded narratives Architecture once awarded
With no real liability for transgression afforded.

So Architecture entered the world of 'whatever'.
It trailed slang faster than fiction's clever
Signs, codes, linguistics, well in fact, a rape
All brought into a tortuous microlandscape.
Notation improved until it was highly possible
To alter all input, and still be irresponsible
For downloading the world, ditto spittoon
The Virtual Conference, Wired up to the balloon.

Hot air it was, though some thought it snow.
Remember everyone who had fortunately passed Go
Arrived at the swimming pool somewhat proactive,
Ready to take confession with Father Interactive.
Of course, they said, knowing the ground underneath,
And speaking, nay mumbling through clenched teeth
Too much talk of shifting the fictive frame,
Until everyone's at it, no one called to blame.
Abbreviated to SIC. it was possible to revise

Subjectivity and narrative before your very eyes.
Little survived the spell-check progam called *Jargonia*
Someone mentioned song lines, another Patagonia.
Was this in the Auschwitz Software, no one quite sure
How to think, even what any of this meant anymore.
A movement, an ideology, a theory, wag or a witticism
Could it really mean Somnambulant Incessant Criticism?

eleven **Sonnets Boom**

As the seminar supper proceeded slowly,
No one saw what was really being done
To the reader underneath in the name of fun.
Near famous though backgrounds lowly
Architects rushed to be considered holy
To interact, so to appear flushed
Meant the project's subtext was solely
Awkward, insecure, many blushed.
Until Johnson entered in quite a flap
Whilst both Harry and Frank quietly sat
Creased linen suit, cigar and panama hat.
Said the immortal Johnson: Cut the Crap
    Architecture need no longer ever fear
    One more artful meta-grumbling year.

When in the chronicle of wasted time,
Who envisaged what? Harry or Frank asked
The sonnet boom will boom again, rhyme
Into the liquid crystal it so basked.
But it's back to business in the plain.
Father Interactive with Shakespeare we cross
To avoid dear incomprehensibility's pain.
The next few years will be such a loss,
Orson will step out as the Lady of Shanghai

Challenging everyone one and all:
Make my Millennium, Punks, shoot and lie!
Go on Architect, raise the call.
      Nothing mattered was our cynical de-light.
      We have eyes to wonder but little left to fight.

If there be nothing new, but that which is,
Is it worth it to attempt to skew
Grand invention's labour and remain amiss
From the spent spectacle of God's few
Who cooled off philosophy's pain
With the anxiety of falsification
And made glory possible again
By opting for their own interpretation.
This ensured that authenticity again took over
Dominant and dominating aesthetic worth,
The self-doubting spectre of a *vita nuova*
Disappearance had finally come back to earth.
      Make Architecture from this, an aging Johnson said
      Let's get back to the Encyclopaedia, the one in our head.

Not marble, nor the guilded monument
Pleasure of Architecture, Bliss, and Time.
Nothingness, Johnson said, sufficient content
To outlive such a powerful rhyme,
As he waved into the cathedral womb
Of Grand Central Station at high noon
Frauds . . . this isn't the Cabinet Room
Don't you remember! (Alzheimer soon)
We all made those cardboard wing chairs boom
And just who could sit in such a cutout
Depended upon who could cleverly write,
Fabricate, invent, use their clout
To turn on the fawning critic's spite.

Frank looked blank, turned pale and grey.
The century had never been interpreted this way.

Full many a glorious morning have I seen
Up until this moment, myself in calm control.
Now once outside the Hotel have I been
Architecture's guards, armed on patrol.
Dum dum bullets flying all around,
Virtual direction, heat heat-seeking.
The Crisis Team were about to hound
Erasers bent on sentiment leaking
Anyone caught trying to erase
Last century's baroque-fold
Was committed to a theory phase
They could no longer scaffold.
 Warrior commitment! it was named
 After the angels, it was to be famed.

When to the symposiums of sweet silent thought
After the perturbation of language tease,
Had scraped Architecture off what it sought
Architecture limped, then kicked up with ease
Returned to the cold condition of War.
The classical mask marked on all the Arts
Brought pathos once again to the fore.
Images reawakened, dis-figured into parts.
The soundtrack of the century invented anew.
Viewmaster helmets on a display tatty and bruised
The One-liners had just set up their own crew
In off the piazza where now only ladies cruised
 Looking for toy-joy. Titillation along the Highway
 Architecture's Trash-can Sinatras doing 'My Way'!

twelve **AKIRA**
(Architecture Kept In Raging Anarchy)

It's taken this far to avoid any conclusion
And some will certainly have their favourite lines.
So it's on we continue, prepared to pay the fines
Risking Architecture's greater, lonelier seclusion.

Clearly it must be worth hijacking the rest
Of this lengthy poem, saving it for the novel.
And let's admit, it might be for the best
For we wouldn't really want our Guests to grovel

Amongst purple passages that rant on and on.
So without further ado let's introduce AKIRA.
For Architecture's undoing has now been done
Are we sure we are any the wiser, nay clearer?

Apparently slogan is out and in is the sound byte
Rhyming is favoured so it's a return to the fight:

For winning couplets that the bet hedges
Talk of the threatened and threatening edges

Where anything could happen except the unexpected
Where voting's irrelevant, fools still get elected

To lead Architecture to that point Degree Zero
Where morpho-genesis rules, the spiralling hero

With the permanence of hallucination and death
As something too real now to imagine. Breath

Comes in less sizes than usually found
Only the L, XL, and XXL around.

And despite the world's warning made to itself
Architecture also seriously damages health.

Cigarettes are still pumped endlessly along
The corridors of the Hotel where lizards throng.

Deprived, the Dean sat in the Hotel Lobby
Has all this been nothing more than a simple hobby?

For survival it would surely be crucial hence
To reduce ideas to an acceptable sequence

(No one could mention the word 'narrative' of course
Sound bytes questioned the 'national project' force)

Extremity of sign given the *whatever* once over
The Architecture of Exhaustion, the cliffs of Dover.

Architects in Crisis popped up, trainers without laces
In any of the world's Shakespearean places.

In a bid to have something more to represent
To huff intellectuals losing out to slick content

Incapable of truly discriminating between
Fiction and reality as it was once seen.

Tragedies in architecture now enacted
Through fiction, screen, interacted

Leaving Architecture free to be pursued:
Displacement, angle, architectonically slewed.

No fantasy league meant the death of the Architect
All too real to be entertained. And so defect.

Strangely no medium now strong enough to survive;
Pre-electronic infuriation and irritation alive.

Still to write out a scenario of Gothic scale
The Hill taken over by a Tate Gallery tale

The Thousand Island authorities caught in a thrilling
Reenactment of Deconstruction, detonating, drilling

Exploding all the best buildings with gleeful care.
A suspect claim to elegance, a genteel fare

For the modern history of the last hundred years
On the pretext it eventually fast-forwards fears.

And that virtual versions of monuments past
Are more permanent, and will definitely last.

At least longer than this, the real event;
Invention weak and futile, imagination spent.

The Essentialists rent out the Cabinent Room
They advertise though, a period of immense gloom.

A one-night stand to alight on the truest word
Investing melodrama bit by bit. Quite unheard!

The Digital City is, they fear, they say,
Just there for the taking, Creeps! on its way

Out of sight, round the corner of the Hotel
Don't be fooled, they say, behind the Motel

Ready with the unnecessary plans to splatter
New significance. But what does it matter?

These small penetrating vectors dimly non-sensed,
A discourse scaffolded, bordered, bounded, fenced.

Waiting for the time words need to scrape and clean
Architecture to a timeless reality, honest and mean.

Outside the Cabinet Room the lobby fills up.
Heavy, congested, instant coffee, paper cup.

No one clears out the e-mail come each morning,
Symbol and icon both add to their warning.

Screen savers redesign in total absurdity;
Ruling, unprejudiced, their talent is free

To compete for digital cunning with one another
Leaving the Brave Inaction Heros rashly to smother

Their charges of another aesthetic conspiracy:
A propagandist plot, a joke, the damnest tyranny

To make Architecture hands-free, without building
A clean, lucid sentence, without further gilding.

But Frank sees in this an outrageous ploy
Hypocritical, never himself quite that coy

Reminds him of the Grand Old Shaman, Frank L. Wright
He'd go home, he says, if he only knew the right

Way to turn, Gin or Tectonics, but that really is the rub;
No direction home, he says, have to stay in the Club.

We have suddenly forgotten what this was all about
Was it not AKIRA, Architecture's last shout?

For the drinks before, in the bar, time is served
And the sonnet delivered, like the fast ball curved.

. . . .

A Commentator arrives, just down for the weekend,
Unaware of the creases in the linen suits
And the wear signs in the wing-chair flutes,
Says that words will automatically extend
To suit immediacy of their own anxiety.
Doesn't know what all the fuss is about,
All these skulls walking around with piety;
Helmets won't prevent, won't stem loyalty's rout.
Obvious through their neat Snoopy bow ties
Concealed, the past's sublime, ever so slightly under
Their angora sweaters computer patterned. No wonder
Allegiances netted, webbed on the wordly wise
    Oh and as for the title, the novel, let me see
    Architecture Kept (*Alive*) in Raging Anarchy.

thirteen **Nulla Verba**

Stealth is no longer charm,
The future, one of some alarm,
Is on automatic pilot set
To the Fourth World inlet.
Lax it is, and Lax is where
The plane touches down unaware
That the Virtual Journeying will
Have to come to a joystick standstill.
But Architecture's future, it wobbles on
The steely sum of indecision on indecision
So satiated with prattle, indecent
Insecurity itself so wilfully recent.

Charm is openness, watch it fly!
Stupidity, progresses by the by,
Communicated at the speed of light.
The new *Imamology* arrives overnight
And before anyone can quite identify it.
Makes a television programme to wit,
From the very airport, humid and hot
The message—*Nulla verba*—shot
Across the screens like a lecture
Predictably reading 'Ditto: Architecture!'
Fast enough for them to repeat:
Complexity minus cusp replete
For the simplistic agenda to win
Surfaces painted over, deftly, in
Fifteen versions of the palimpsest;
Rhyme, couplet, ode and sonnet incest.

A silk anorak slips in the Jumbo Jet
Sleek, handsome, exquisite you can bet
This is Architecture as it is found
In the sixties, Timeless Science, unbound.
Whilst in the Euro-snack Cafeteria,
More Digital items on the 'Ateria'
Euro-Porky and Euro-tasty
Tempt the Jury members into hasty
Decisions about this urgent rise
To respect architectural lies.
The *Flâneur*, in crumpled linen cream
Still narrating his digital dream;
Hails one of those, the yellow taxis—
Take me to the Paris-St. Petersburg axis—
Has all but given up the nine-hole course
Of Architecture's ghost discourse.
Achtung Architecture! and hey they all do
Whilst the *Blaguer*, a distant type, all voodoo

Digitalised, fitted out, put on hold;
Matching dementia, cartoon-behaviour mode.

The author, sitting, lonely, waiting for the Final,
Still insists on listening to Radio Vinyl,
Attends the fitting session at his peril.
Oh the eye patch. Ah hah, cap'n, it's Errol!
But the Stand-up Architect delays
Heroic Heroism's final days,
Until the screen blurs and burns,
Programmed as it is in turns
To catch up with itself and hic
Using the latest dittographic
Models of the Morphic Garden.
Whilst Architects up from Ardennes
Dress in their usual neon hard hat,
Leaving their brogues outside on the mat,
Enter gingerly through the crystal maze
Speechless at this new architectural haze.

In their torn resin-soaked raincoats,
Suspended theory watches as it floats.
Held up at the border of the Leakage Zone,
Each takes out a mobile phone.
Brain survives, liquid crystals claw
Knocking on the millennial door:
Thump and thud with the fidget-sponge
Try again, thump, thud and lunge
Our Hard Hat looks on in dismay
Can this be our Century's relay?
As the offical hour approaches,
Outside all the tourist coaches
Arrive and turn over their load
To the Third Millennium's code.
Nulla verba, that huge huge tome
Flying finns and burning chrome.

Archobabble and anxiety,
Even pre-electronic piety
Twitching, surely still alive
The tongue now in cheek. Five
Fingers firmly skewed inside
With nowhere else left to reside,
Father and Son play shadow themes
Whilst the Age of Oedipus screams
Step on Father's artificial head
Let in another before he's dead.

The Grand Clickster heavy with breath
Arranges an orbital balloon death
Size XXL through genetic breakdown,
As the Anarchists fight for the crown
To rock Greenwich Observatory once more,
Without tripping up through the floor
And detonating, feet overlapped,
The device to the body strapped.
Suicide architectural Bombers rise
Give weak Architects their alibis.

So impatient now to erase the archive
So pleased in the Oedipal Zone to survive
They merge and take over from the Digital
Genetic Engineering Architectural Fidgetal!
Outrageous sentiment slips through and through
On its way to becoming normal. Really? Phew!
And yet, what is out there, what do we lack?
The screen chorus, the first to answer back:

What interest is there in replying,
If talking is indistinct from lying.
And the tongue can but be weak
Puts Architecture further inside the cheek?

fourteen **A Criticaster**

With that low cunning, which in fools supplies
And amply too, the place of being wise.

Nulla verba! Architects, stomachs, blood pressure
And flamed kidneys now define this leisure.

All held in by the museum electronic,
Their rise and fall, crumble and tonic.

A distorted, dismembered, dis-figured play
All the time navigating the lonely Highway

To ecstasy, a charisma by-pass;
Stop to every arrival now so crass.

To stop here, *Nulla verba*, now
To stop those open mouths going 'wow'

Would be to insist on losing hope,
To direct the future and Architecture's scope,

When we have been so happily led
To the grand abandon in the head.

. . . .

The Hotel Architecture, digitalised, cool
Swimming pool lights on, awaits the fool,

Sits back for the ceremony's start;
A redefinition of Theory's part

In the History of Modernity writ
By the scholars, hip to the New Crit

Of situating the swimming pool where
Other icons can now but stare.

Without this nothing would develop,
Rapid Eye Movement tediously envelop

Architectural virtue unawares
In disseminating vice's snares.

Your vehicle of conveyance, choose:
Mountain bike or Snow-board cruise

Avanti, Architecture! go go go
As the Hoodwinkers meet Godot

The hero of the Tour de France,
Waiting ecstatically in a trance

For the Anti-aesthetic all over again.
Dittography the name of this new game.

fifteen **The Ancient Witness**

From Mandelbrot they took out the cream.
But only Benoit saw it clearly and from a dream
Turn into the dullness of a sly prognosis,
And the invention of applied Morpho-genesis.

Not far from the epicentre of the earthquake
Decentred Architecture Victims scheme and shake
The Hotel Architecture flat to the ground.
Still no one claims to have heard a sound.

As the cockroach research into shadows began,
'Tread on the head', the limpid chorus ran.

Scripted on the Net and long long lost
To computer-aided programmes. What a cost!

Little fibre-optic fluid in the spaces,
As miniature as tiny Gulliver's laces;
Making architecture from the intestinal
Displacement now on track, so unfinal.

. . . .

Dum Dum is now a whole city, faking nectars,
A partial totality, complete with all those missing vectors.
Problematized meaning, made a sentence once more
As the Architectural Bull, perturbed by grammar's score

Unmeant itself with metaphysics underachieved,
Leaves the doubting disbelievers so calmly relieved.
Fortunate that they had the faith and nerve
To remain outside this discursive verve.

They insisted on remaining displaced and dis-figured,
The tiredness of the world's words triggered
Again into a repetition. No one would say lies.
But it would certainly make Viktor de-familiarise

And turn over in his own damp grave
His own death and seduction save.
Too late, though no one could stop
The Hoodwinkers latest conceptual flop.

About Digitopolis and continuous unrest
How the proud move, upset, are blessed.
Gone were the angora plain, and in
Were those patterned chipped versions thin.

The Super-cipher was already over-leaning
To empty out one more Architecture as meaning.

Identifier, instructor, conductor and informer
Defender to all men, something even warmer

The Ancient Witness advised, high and tall
Said that rebirth had to come to us all.
And come quickly, if this thinness was not
To overwhelm the planet in an unseemly knot

Of non-sense communicated at net-pace.
Beyond Architecture we were now in cyber space
Heading for the Fourth World. Trying
To whisper, wake up, desist from lying.

The waxed fruit cannot be told apart
From real fruit anymore. Simulacra's art!
And wax is now genetically implanted
With architectural goodness easily decanted.

Whether they wanted me dead or alive,
The Ancient Witness said, all a clever skive,
Their tongues always wagged, mouths saying one thing
Their eyes rolled and surfed, other glories to bring.

Our sympathy for the Ancient Witness so warm;
For how much had he taught in play's gentle form?
And could he mind that they had Architecture repeated,
And if he himself felt rejected if not defeated?

And from his work, his bulls and thought they made,
What game the contemporary moment now played?
They all angled ever so carefully for his loyalty
Without offering him one single royalty.

A greater talent I fear we will not see,
For death will fabricate this history.
And he will be lost to this fake time
Instead of hailed, Master in his prime.

Part Five The Logics of Re-enchantment

one **The Logics of Re-enchantment**
(Songs From)

The more Architecture begins to tell
Its own story in this ill-mannered hell,
The easier it is to reverse it, to whiten it
To turn it inside out once more, to heighten it.

Not a sentence to be found amongst the lizardry,
Not a screen saved by its own wizardry.
Not a language but language error and flaw
Not an Architecture but architectural law.

Not an Opera House of stunning 'fold' and 'peel'
But an ambience we live with, quite unreal.
Dubious from its origin, surely one big modern plot
Knowing just what to locate, and where, in the blind spot.

The joker in the pack, the *Zero Degree Zero*;
Enter our old friend, the Architectural Hero,
As the dummy in bridge, necessary to the game
Redundantly living on in the pain of fame.

Deliriously lost to any fixed meaning, we fawn
At the Logics of Re-enchantment about to be born.
Ditto today, tomorrow, Architecture in between fall,
Dismiss Oedipus's bull and narrative's last call.

What then has love really got to do with it, pray?
Head for the swimming pool, absolutely no delay.
Whisper it, we are no longer the public square
We are also no longer the piazza out there.

And Architecture is no longer the enigma of the campo,
For we seek a quite different Architectural *sampo.*
So forget the brief affair chronicled in the Motel,
We are the illuminated swimming pool of the Hotel.

Through us pass histories, fictions, bits and bytes,
No structure can fly both Savage and Salvaged kites.
So make your minds up, Crystal Palace or Cordoba,
Or then the sponsored balloon, dome and a virtual fly-over

From Clermont-Ferrand to the west of Millau,
Jasmine rice, Basmati, Uncle Norman's or pillau.
2001 a Space Odyssey it might be;
Or Euston Arch, the Revival's apogee.

Even Hawksmoor, Lutyens and Christoper Wren
Could and will come, before the neon digital pen
Wipes out history from under our blocked noses
Backing up the hearse, only to sniff the roses.

Just as off the flat earth of the millennium trip
Confidence and credibility on the plasma drip.
Ditto: Nothing outside except this XXL breath
And Architecture once more sentenced to death.

Exonerating the world of inaccuracy seemed futile
So yet another conference organised, deemed Ditto-style.
And another level of spectacle soon in grave danger
Of emerging from the turbulent cradle in the manger.

The survival of an idea, messianic and sovereign
Without limit when fashion came to haunt, hoverin'
Allowing nothing to be completed except history;
The selfsame that runs the risk of digital mystery.

Bring back the original, in its shocking colours,
Charge at the entrance, accept only dollars.
If the Elgin Marbles has been such a tease
The journalist is right, return the peerless frieze.

Go for the Absolutist view, back to the start;
After ripping out the lungs, stop at the heart
For Architecture in pieces, that we can recognise
Perverse as ever, beyond any imaginable prize.

Testified uncertain, this other frissoned tease
Were we fond of neologisms, of the oxymoron's wease,
We would stage and decline in history's state
We would age and define Architecture's precious stalemate.

A spidership, a hyphen-ology, symbolic lore
Endgame, to loosen the theory, nothing more.
Simply the day comes, the rose yearns for the kiss,
When Architecture wants to achieve no more than this.

No further clarity in its false messages and tics,
Nulla verba, its atrociously hijacked meta-physics.
No more the theatre of emotions, lightness smote
The darkness of an Architecture outside the throat.

The tongue not language, and definitely not meaning,
A certain art, of no more nor less ethical leaning.
And as for spectacle, nothing if not a *feinter* trace
To trip over its significance and re-commence apace

The Logics of Re-enchantment, one two three
For at least a fifteen percent bonus-packed fee.
At the end of the day, the Guest Lecturer said
It's all about context, content and dread.

Forget the matter-of fact ring,
The solid properties we bring
To an otherwise arbitrary existence,
With devastatingly boring persistence.

There is always need for an extra exuberant tome
Of lavish abstraction for the scholars to comb.
This time to reveal, superstructure's turbulence,
The excess of any rational project; damn indolence

Taken to its extreme. As back in the Digital Lounge
The machines record whatever Theory on the scrounge.
The Guest Lecturer finished, adjusted the screen,
The technician, bored, inserted the next in the machine.

No one spoke, no one lectured, no one was there.
No discrimination, unprejudiced listening everywhere.
So beastly correct, this inventory of our daily life:
The war of tastes looks set on this, continued strife.

Architecture, that haunting accommodator of continuity,
With digital integration the measure of its acuity;
It is time, gently, before the end, to cut the lines down
Go for rhyme and some reason, reduce the reader's frown

This beastly poem has sadly become an era's chore.
Yet each day, wry non-sense unearths more, and more
Injustice to a discipline so much on the move
That even the unnamed architect of the Louvre

After a Virgin flight with ginandtonica
Opts for a commission with Arquitectonica.
So rats will leave just as sonnets boom;
Anything to hold not to the contemporary gloom.

The Grand Insinuator is new on the scene,
As are the linen covers now freshly clean.
Forget reality! Movement not negation
Will forever instruct this integration.

Sent to subvert, out on the prowl
Virtuality bends, reality cries foul!
Contamination, interference, they softly shout,
Not the shifting ground we are speaking about.

Fixed distinctions have always been wrong
Firm foundations sold out unrest for a song.
Oh *Firmitas*, Oh *Venustas*, Oh *Uticitas*
Virgin Atlantic, sky bar, of course it has!

The Grand Insinuator was quickly shown the door.
The truly great and great again began to look poor.
When freed from the uncertainties of history
Altering the screen was no longer quite that mystery

They all talked about at The MoMA,
Sadly rhyming not with coma, but comma!
Ah not now, Architecture is about to alter
Yet again, impossible to fail but will it falter

As it leans to take the *Compagneiro*'s hints
Seduced by espresso and those zero mints.
The *Campagneiro* wasn't really one to act,
Nor condemn Theory to the dominion of fact

But to placate Theory there was a little abcess,
A subtext to exhume from the project's excess,
Just in time for the holy resurrection gang
The winning foreclosure sign to hang

On all those ideologies neatly trapped,
Stoned, saturated. Where equivalence sapped
The energy out of the very thought
Of Architecture, scanned, sold and bought!

two **The Ballad of Asterisque and Archetypal**

      Asterisque
Such Architecture, oh such perturbation
No more a mockery, read the dissertation.

      Archetypal
No one outlasts the appalling Anti-hero leader
This ghost pales, becomes the Hollywood Reader.

      Asterisque
You mean you begrudge Architecture, all its leisure
And that blissful moment it takes its own pleasure?

      Archetypal
Yes, progress and enlightenment is reversed, undone
Modernity merely defrocked and renamed in eternal fun.

      Asterisque
A semantic trap, we must admit more than a touch overawed
National projects in the last century never quite so flawed.

      Archetypal
But still, Asterisque, we shouldn't be exactly that hard
There's still originality and modesty out on the Boulevard.

      Asterisque
Semantics always did pose—problematically—the issue
The confusion of styles became brave edifice's tissue.

Archetypal
You mean Architecture gained its final, infinite access
To ecstasy and unmeaning by this interactive excess?

Asterisque
Yes, co-habitation and co-option, those unhappy trolls
Tortured vocabulary, worked overtime like neon dolls.

Archetypal
Hell and fire, Asterisque, you can't have it all ways
Architexture, intertexture for all remaining days!

Asterisque
But to order things once more, is this then the Grand Aim,
Against the Anti-hero, a sanctified catastrophic claim?

Archetypal
No, but meaning has of course always been precariously so
Revokable, reversible, interchangable. That we all should know!

Asterisque
But the architectural discourse now forever incomplete
Leaves us shuffling elegantly on patent-leather feet.

Archetypal
Well frankly it's just as well, to shut down and keep
The Ballroom unblemished; let our exhausted guests sleep.

Asterisque
Yes, but what help this, if we sleep the hours of the Dead;
No further discourse on survival, our nostalgias fed?

Archetypal
Pause Asterisque, go back please to Rudyard Kipling's Ah!
Erase, rewind to the point where you lost interest. Blah!

Asterisque
All you have done this century, Archetypal, admit it, is cruise
Just like all the others, your will and power to the Surfers lose.

Archetypal
Oh and you are much better, running off the edge
Like the Merry Pranksters on San Francisco's ledge?

Asterisque
You cruised the world's knowledge for easy hints and clues.
Now, since falling off, you Archetypalists have the blues.

Archetypal
Returning to the edge of the land. Flat-earthers we became.
But we hang in there, on the wave, like you just the same.

Asterisque
Oh you never did understand Architecture's site and reason;
It shifts along the crest, undecidable poetry for any season.

Archetypal
Yes, over the fold and peel, into the vocabulary of unrest.
Architecture reinvented for itself: such untimely pest!

Asterisque
Pester power, really, a discipline you should not mock.
Terrified of the flirtatious, you've become an old crock.

Archetypal
All red and bleary-eyed, there will come the morning
Then you'll realise Architecture must heed our warning.

Asterisque
But there has only ever been one treatise over time
Architecture and asterisks forever intertwine!

Archetypal
From those breaks in language, the noble and the absurd?
You will always weaken yourself by wanting the last word.

Asterisque
You missed out the trivial, the magnificent and the moronic,
The pompous and the ridiculous, the gestalt and the tectonic!

Archetypal
All coming into contact in environments virtually so pure?
You must be kidding to think you've got us pinned onto the floor.

Asterisque
Oh, they will be used as grammatical models, you wait and see:
For the next millennium, simulacra and synchronicity.

Archetypal
I'll have no more of this, I'm heading for the door
Virtually Architecture, like language, slewed once more.

Asterisque
Yes Archetypal, go. But remember there's not that much to fear
Lately at the American Bar, things aren't really that queer.

Archetypal
Always redistributed for the Master's narrative, you fake!
The one that *tells* better than all others. Give me a break!

Asterisque
Schooling be damned, you'll see, we'll ride along the waves
If the site, the import of Architecture's Bull this saves.

Archetypal
Babble gives to prattle, your academic death is near,
If the Digital Lounge this discipline begins to steer.

Asterisque
The attractive errors of others, surely you can't mean.
You're lost on the Highway you haven't even seen.

Archetypal
Not even a ribbon of infra-language. Oh come on now,
Undressing Flaubert at the trendy linguist's pow-wow!

Asterisque
You missed out Saussure, the arbitrary, but never you mind
Perforated discourse wasn't ever the issue of your kind.

Archetypal
Dismantling, deconstructing without rendering it all
Meaningless, unreadable you mean? You've really got the gall!

Asterisque
Yes! Language cutting itself free, at the moment the trap door
Is released by the Executioner and falling through the floor . . .

Archetypal
To a hell of our own making! Don't tell me, you double-fake!
Architectural small change only, buildings on the make.

Asterisque
This could go on forever, neither of us will give way
So subtle, so discriminating, charlatans will have their say.

Archetypal
So light is the slowness, so gentle is the disruption,
So unchanged are things in this aesthetic corruption.

Asterisque
As they appear to be and have, indeed, always appeared to be.
So nearly untenable the Symposium wraps up, Dittographically!

Archetypal
In a series of keynote speeches, just like it was before
Architecture, the most impossible project! Bore! Bore! Bore!

Asterisque
Archetypal, you know, I'm beginning to like you more and more
I want you to explain to me what Faked Discontinuity is for?

Archetypal
Well, it's what controlled violation really represents.
If you favour mimesis, then favour Georgian crescents.

Asterisque
Voilà, Architecture imitating itself and our persistent unrest
Welcome to the Nightclub Brio, at Architecture's grand bequest.

Archetypal
Asterisque, I too like you more, no longer one of my foes
Plagiarised to stand on your own, touching on your toes.

Asterisque
Just at the moment of excess, those halogen lights beaten.
That skewered concrete, stringy like the veal uneaten.

Archetypal
So let's agree to disagree in this our charming rhyming battle;
Architecture to mean again must finally transcend all this prattle.

Asterisque
Yes! Architecture becoming itself infinitely is rather tired
As are the attempts to overflow, outlaw itself, be hot-wired.

Archetypal
Oh and through the doors of a lost language, through the dust,
The skipped passages of all the books read in uncertain lust.

Asterisque
The skipped passages in buildings aimlesslesly wandered through
In theories extended, seduced with little fiat left but to skew.

Archetypal
Living permanently, the imaginary universe next door,
No longer ideological, spills and burns on the Lounge floor.

Asterisque
Decreeing foreclosure, now I understand the term
Never simple, never easy, to be clear, concise and firm.

Archetypal
So one last journey amongst the wing chairs and chandeliers,
Back to the Teatro Cervantes, that opera house in tiers.

Asterisque
To proceed towards its own contradictions, a dialogue, No!
Running risk of aggression, blackmail, definitely no undertow.

Archetypal
You really think, Asterisque, you have the architectural bottle
To return to Alberti, to Vitruvius, even back to Aristotle?

three **My Heart Leaps Up**

It is time, always was, to go as fast as we can
But I fear my awkward rhyme, like my low tan,
Is bland, English, wan and analytically tame.
This beastly poem potentially quite the same.

Interface is now the almighty word
Spotted, common, an unrare bird.
The screen open to metaphor's rule
To surf, to morph, oh so cool.

As Architecture's representation splinters
Collapsing viewpoints, multiple winters
Are all in store, what a sight!
At seven hundred and twenty megabyte.

A provocative fault line, I know
More de-limits will this paradox grow
Into one huge internal discourse.
As Lloyd's electra-glided blue bourse

Is launched with mischievous glee
On its maiden voyage far out to sea,
The scholarship student anxiously waits
For the liquorice vodka to arrive in crates

At The Hotel Architecture Bar just in time
To prevent Frank's imitation of Harry Lime.
Too sweet for the playboys, this vodka cup
Needs a touch of lizard to freshen it up.

The Logics of Re-enchantment now apace
The atrium collapses, and another interface
Blamed for this inter-coursed rubble:
Hubble bubble, tectonics and trouble.

Cosmic pragmatism is all we hear,
As the end of the poem draws near.
And the A-team led by Theodor Adorno
Is accused once more of the fragmented Porno

Effect of despair and doom on low culture,
Masquerading as the VIP vulture.
And the B-team led by Maurice Blanchot
Never seen but in that sixty-nine tableau:

Inavowable Community without a home
Steely rival to the aging Club of Rome.
To go by some, they go by Rorty
As if, like me, when we're forty

We're ousted by the cry: Get shorty.
I know, a fourth rhyme, naughty, naughty!
Why oh why did we bother? So ungifted,
Talent sadly lacking, we merely lifted

Theories and ideas outside the word
To be upstaged by a computer nerd
Fluent in the hypermediated universe
Ready with jargon, hot with the curse.

Leaves you wondering why the hell
You ever bothered to ring the godless bell
At The Hotel Architecture up on seven;
That simulacrum some call heaven.

It has been relatively easy after all
Those truly madly gullible can but fall
Into the total essential concept Go!
Leave the fractals for another show.

Migraine splinter! Oh fragmenting world
Into the foetal position now curled
The welcome Logics of Re-enchantment
Firmly ground, firmly emplanted

In Architecture's cool de-schooling.
Listen up, we've not been fooling.
Unlearning soon to find favour,
In-your-face, something to savour.

four **What the Hell!**
(A Vocabulary Primer from the Solitary Reaper)

Asked how it felt to be
What it felt like to see
Things so peculiarly
Wedged between the three
Poems that make up the primer
For the ambitious climber
The Dead Author of Mantras Digital
All things Architectural-fidgetal
Said, What the hell, who cares!
Vocabulary is there for any who dares
To take on during this unstable era
Words devalued as often as the lira.

. . . .

And the new one, on the Slick Media shelves
Software Duchamps not Magrittes to Ourselves

Though the Publisher preferred Fairy
The Author felt it quite contrary

Software Fairies to Ourselves
Turns us into miniature elves

Especially as in the *feuille de chou*
From Silverlake Boulevard came the clue

Ignatius Loyola's new *tromp l'oeil*
Citing Pozzo, Architecture oh so coy.

De-territorialisation, a word quite lost
Subject sadly to its de-colonised cost.

Re-situating held such fragile verve,
Lost its own epistemological nerve.

Nothing was more exciting
Than the fever for re-citing

Representation, a condition queer
Bordering on the far and near

Long before dis-semination came
To make the Hierophant a family name.

Counterhegemonic strategies arrived
At the Hotel daintily, so neatly contrived

Were one-arm bandits impossible to lose,
Amidst the screens they love and cruise.

Cigarettes were lit in the pause;
No one either for effect or cause.

Alterity, now there's a perfect suiting.
Trimmed, stitched, a disembodied rerouting

Of those truisms that get up the nose
Architecture, therefore I am! I suppose.

Vocabulary like an addicted Microserf
Gets the scholars across Pont-Neuf

On and over into Musée d'Orsay
To an exhibition of Sartre's *Nausée*

Pages, notes and lots of lies
Turned into Existentialism's alibis.

I was, though, unable to escape this bind
Never leaving melancholia so far behind

That even now this uncomplicated sense
Of origins takes me stuttering hence

To the Anti-aesthetic, muddled as we know;
Desperately incoherent feelings for snow.

. . . .

    So onto an architecture sonnet we should go
    Strangers to ourselves, fourteen lines to create
Nothing stunning, allowing death to hyper-mediate
The sense of loss, that once burning glow.
Faire soul in this Media Age so shin'd thou bright
And made all eyes with wonder thee beholde
Till ugly discourse depriving us of light
Into the yawning gap thee did enfolde
Out of the margins, what shall remain
Of all this babble, now seated on the Highway?
Where information snipes from out of the byway
Something simple that such reasons raine,
    Supplementing all quests for the grail
    Architecture's trophies hung on the nail.

. . . .

The sonnet over for a short while
Let's return to simpler style.

Hybridity, now there's one up and running,
From the start without all that punning.

One that mars the magic-realist card
By hysterically trying a little too hard

To reground the slow historical harvest;
Singularly unattractive. A futile quest

To prise the dullest repertoire apart,
Like the kernel through displacement's heart.

Ah, displacement, a word so often used
No apology for with Architecture fused

The Hotel knows just how much of this
With the tectonic gives gin the hiss.

Temptation leans over a little too far
Invites oblivion, we'll need to take the car

If we are to arrive safely yet again
By avoiding to take the unreliable plane.

Philosophy into Architecture flows like tears
To rhyme not with softwares but fears.

The Hotel's imaginary, you made it all up
You should apologise, you horrid cur, you pup!

A re-inscription is not enough, no never
Has the B-team met someone, anyone, so clever

To shift the configurations out of site
Of the Architectural Bull and to make such light

Banter along the way?
You're sure to pay

For failing to attend the need
Inviting such deconstructive greed.

And you can forget that Professorship
If you insist on such unhip lip

Architecture owes you nothing, didn't ask
To prepare any essay, a thankless task

In no less than five thousands words
On the diasporic identities of the Kurds.

Forget those words, return to ambiguity
Seven types at least before the gratuity

Can be paid for turning up with your wife
And child. That symbolic flux of everday life.

five **The Solitary Reaper**
(Suitably Coy)

So tell Horrid Author, your career
And should you mistakenly fear
Be sure, don't leave out a thing
You know we have many ways to bring
All the ugly past to the fore.
If you resist to go to the core,
Disguising sadness with a digital blip
Remember what uses this microchip
Embedded in your ankle deep.

So don't try signifying on the cheap.
And don't whatever you do fall
For the easy self-referral call

We've had quite enough of those
In Architecture's narrative shows.

Haven't you yet heard or seen
The Logics of Re-enchantment's been
On the agenda for quite a while
Or are you losing your style.
Where have you been all these nights?
Did you not see, so dimmed the lights
To announce error disrobed, entry free
To the Millennium's Misunderstanding party.
A celebration, a dome, the fetish of the new
Whilst fireworks splutter, ejaculate and spew
Knowledge you'll return, once more
Like that abused, undressed whore.

*(And so as the Digital fuses fail
The fireworks fall to no avail
And a sonnet creeps in on us frail
Rhymes insistent to make Coleridge pale)*

. . . .

Look up and there in Casio's silky Digital
At Ignatius St. Loyola's gorgeous infinite ceiling
Straight at the edge, then curved what feeling
Splendrous satin, the Architectural-fidgetal
Backed up by the real Padre Andrea Pozzo
Beyond sight, beyond open mind
The vendor outside, mustard with chorizo
Guidebook lagging far behind.
In Architecture's newest grammar
The flat one, in the piazza gone
Under the vengeful hammer
Under the blade, one by one by one.

Distanced now the rhyme for greater effect
Just what from digits could you really expect?

And from a beastly poem such as this
The Grammar of Architecture's bliss?
Hold on, really, why the grand invite
To a seminar if just to fly a kite
Of Savaged or Salvaged Mind
Rappel à l'ordre, or like kind?
A timeless, timebound moment invent,
Mythical scholarship to subvent.
Or supply a destiny for the West
As fate frames Architecture's best
Leaving lesser talents high and dry
Whilst Promise endowed, queues up to fly.

All this suggested by our Academy Leader
Who still hints at the Death of the Reader.
Don't fall for it, I would quietly advise
Safer it is, provocative and even wise
Not to achieve excess unbound
Or leave language lying around.
By all means turbulence reveal,
Certainty and partial totality conceal
But to become the very latest on-line
No more, no less, like aperitif wine
Architecture in the digital lounge swills.
And through its teeth running spectacle kills
For its position; a site of ongoing power,
Whilst the meek rivals in falsehood cower.

(Are we sure just which Vitruvian pair
Will lead us to renewed charm and flair?
Or will the ascendent paradigm appear
Out of the sonnet, irreducibly queer?)

. . . .

Lindemans Bin Sixty-five
Southeastern Australia Chardonnay
Redemption now strangely alive
An atonal assembly, wouldn't you say?
Hardly that, hardly metropolitan,
Redemption never more than luck.
Give us more, only if you can
Now it's time to end this book.
Oh, that's hasty, hold on there
Foreclosure's an acquired talent
Taught by intellect's vernacular
All this meaning, damn it, meant.
    Ditto Architecture at the old Colon Hotel
    Manners more fitting to a chronicled motel.

Forget the wine now into the pasta
Usurp falsity all we can
Means we eat that bit faster
And learn of well-situated man.
Disembodied knowledge now aside
The rhyme it turns with the tide
As the excrement hits the oriental fan.
And moved upwards into attic-level
Theory, its very location,
We find ready to bedevil
Frisch's fire-raisers on vocation:
    Attack useless, enemy down and weak
    Petrol has begun to spring a leak

Trickles into docksides and brogues.
Architecture now so thick with rogues

So isn't it better we return,
Logical the imperative to learn.

No one matches anymore need;
The heat is on. All the more greed!

So so easy with happy digital flame
Smoke without fire will be to blame.

For the Hotel in its ashes strewn
Found, the remains of the symposium tune

And so we leave somewhat blind
This poem of a very different kind.

Sonnet. Ode. Couplet, Song and Free Verse
A healthy attempt, though some doubtless curse,

To discuss Architecture's pain and plight
In its closing second-millennial fight

With sponsors, clients, dreamers too,
Bankers, athletes all without a clue.

For status, credibility now so low
Into the Third Millennium we must go.

And take Architecture's visions slowly there
With Gestalt and Tectonics also fare

Utopia with handbag, matching dementia
Nothing like the usual, boring 'cementia'.

And if we cannot stomach such a return
Then from scratch, Architecture must learn.

And now I guess, Dear Reader, you want to know
Where came this abysmal upsetting atonal flow.

And how on earth, no one put a stop
To a project insane as a spinning top.

The green one with lights, and Lambada
The one your daughter found much harder

To keep spinning, than these ditties
A thousand apologies, a thousand pities!

Welcome to The Hotel Architecture, why oh why
Was it not curtailed, instead a book to buy?

Then the postcard came through the door,
Time for the doorknob to break once more.

Message, Simple! Fulbright Done
Still waiting for the sun.

Which is more for Architecture we can now say,
Quixote punished for all this play,

And the Horrid Author probably maligned
For attempting entertainment of this kind.

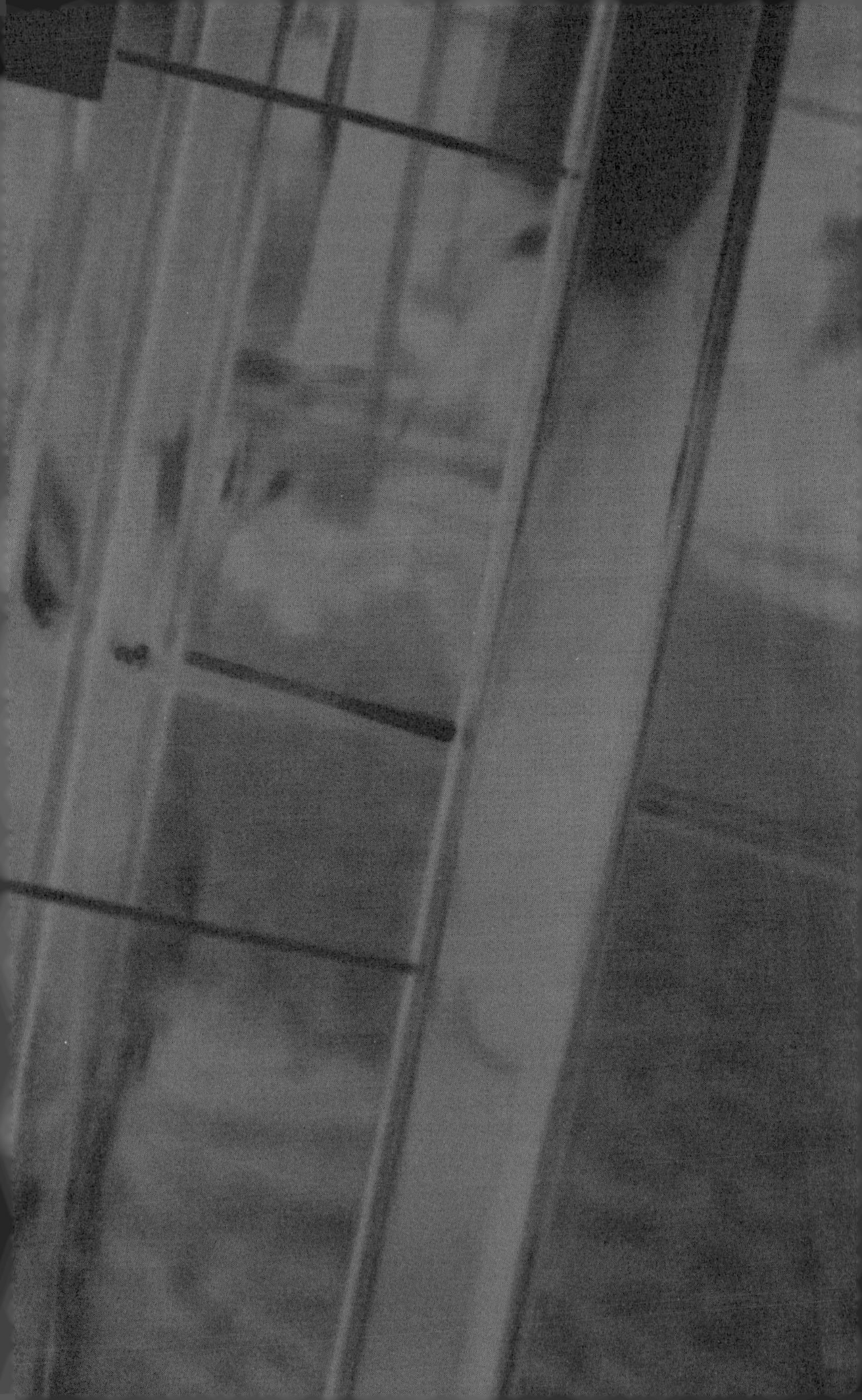

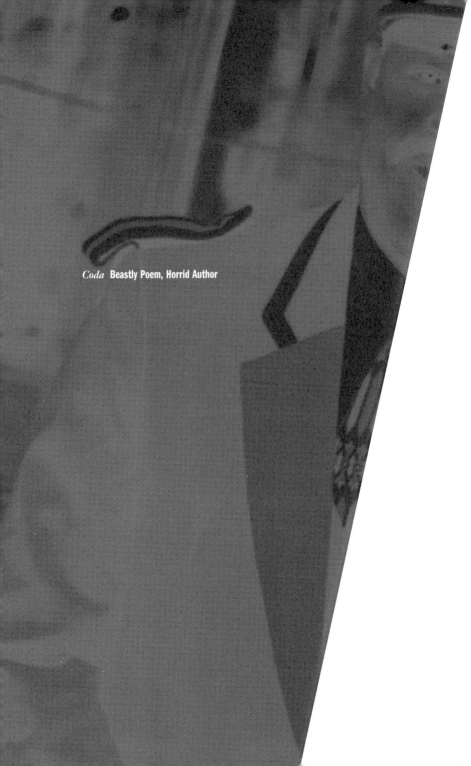

Coda **Beastly Poem, Horrid Author**

Whilst in India, the first book came
A weighty tome, with a fitting name;
Writing Architecture, largish format
No better to some than a stippled doormat.
Awarded, feted, requests followed one by one
To repeat these thoughts, see them undone.
Until one arrived during Easter rain
To visit Latin America, not Spain.
Alfred E. Norton, addressed by hand;
We hope you could visit our land.

Dressed in jeans, matching tweed
The India Within had fulfilled its need
So into Buenos Aires light
Of luggage lost in flight
The nervous author watched the plane
Refuel in Rio and out again.
Sitting next to Sean Connery's stand-in
The Highlander film he'd had a hand in.
Flying down to Rio was not the plan
Engine dicky, said the Service Man.
So on the tarmac they had to stay
A bomb scare still the order of the day.
Until two hours later, engine fine
Plane to runway and off a second time.
Only to find the reception bored, arrival late
They'd all gone home, wouldn't wait.

No hotel, no money, nothing known
Left Alf thinking, should he have flown?
When a bed was kindly proposed.
The stand-in from Miami predisposed
To spend the night high on coke
Leaving Alf, amongst the glue to poke
For credit cards all together stuck,
And marvel at his stroke of luck.

So the beastly poem began its life
Along with reluctant author's Indian wife.
Married quickly, almost on the run
As the saying goes: In the sun
Mad dogs. And Englishmen.
Dal Lake. Oh at least ten
House boats all in line.
Honeymoon, Memsahib and wine
Until the marriage veered astray
To Punjab with the poem for the day.
Where up in Chandigarh Alf finally knew
Architecture, neither false nor true,
Came poking angrily for crumbs
Amidst the riots, failed its sums.
Brought troops out onto the street
Before baton-charging by the elite.

Earlier in Sofia, the Carnival had begun
Alf, at that time, an Also-ran;
A strange International Academy set up,
Gorbachev's glasnost beginning the letup.
When one of the Players did not arrive,
Alf was asked to step in, give them five
Thoughts on Architecture, in order to cater
For the fashion that critics later
Turned into theses, the impossible plot,
Modern/Postmodern. It mattered not.

So Alf delivered a neat off-the-cuff scheme,
Lifting Edmund Leach's Euler dream
Of how cultures use logic to communicate
And other structures by which they mate.
Lévi-Strauss was then no mere name
For Denim's stretched, riveting claim.
In Garrick Club coloured shirt,
Alf convinced a decade flirt

In Architecture's promised bliss
Might not go so remotely amiss.

Just the beginning, unwittingly so
Alf was a hit, an unlikely career in tow.
So in Connaught Circus, round the corner
From Delhi's only named, Finnish sauna
A ticket was stickered up, stop over? Hei hoh!
No problem, Delhi, Bangkok, Singapore and Tokyo.
San Francisco even New York and across
The Atlantic, no cabin-pressure loss.
To *EllOwenDeeOwen*, where on one last leg
An omelette minus the crucial egg
Meant Delhi's heat blasted through
Shattering all but Air India's crew.

And so began the Round-the-world trip
Safer, less provocative than ship.
To a seminar on the West Coast,
Unseemly coffee with morning toast
Whence the first part of the poem
Just like that, *bohème! bohème!*
To Carmel from Monterey
Hovering for the Perrier,
Not so far from the Golden Gate
A quiet arrival somewhat late
Whilst a suitable boy made up verses
Nothing satanic about those curses.
The Schaeffer cleaned, ready for playing,
Took no more than a lifted Polish saying:
Caressing a cat to death!
Written quickly, out of breath.
All about architecture's Fake
Discourse. Do so, cut the cake,

The Chairman said, meaning 'crap'
But ducking out, all in a flap.
Fine, Alf replied gingerly unbowed,
Aching to exit this madding crowd,
But surely couldn't that line read
Anywhichway taken at speed?

From Carmel back to Monterey,
India bypassed on the way.
Then onto Vienna, down to Graz,
Missing out on their version of *Cats*;
To deliver a quick inaugural address
On Film and Arc. Abbreviated stress
Brought in the characters Frank and Harry
Though now Alf wished it had been Larry
Olivier who could have taught a thing or two
About this fractured discipline, splintered zoo.

Still the roghan josh in copper kept
Warm, spiced, alive. No one wept
For Architecture's slow demise,
Preferring those attractive lies
Of discourse, panels and photographs.
See you again, and all the other laughs.
To Hotel Altstadt, this chicanery forced
Alf to exit, disenchanted, of course
Not before by the Sushi a child came
To be confirmed in Venice, the very same
Nadezna Alice Xenia, star
The fastest swimmer by far.

Over to The Hotel Colon, up the stairs, where
In the lobby, Frank had that bemused stare.
Deep, nonplussed, just happened to be here

Where the promising World Architects steer
The discourse this way and that,
By subtle talking through the hat.
No! Stay I won't. Yes, later visiting Gaudi
Before Business Class to Saudi
Where the Guggenheim discuss the 'biz'.
Makes a change after all the 'Diz'
Knee-jerk museum and innovative Catia
Which makes the jury quite the scattier.

Frank laughed and said, Alf you know,
There's more to Architecture than this show
To which Alf could but agree.
Yes Frank, can't they see?
Architecture knows just when to turn
Use the slogan: Burn, Frank, Burn!

Anyplane but this one, go
Anyway it's really time, so
From anyplace but here, Alf departed
Questions unanswered, visions uncharted.
We'll be hearing from you again,
Perhaps Montreal, BA but not Spain.
We need to talk, you have something to say
But naturally, it will have to be another day.
Thank you for coming, so nice so nice
Loved the idea of doing it twice.
And the poem slipped in between
Work on it, publishers are now so keen
To widen our notoriety,
With such eccentric sobriety.

Rant, be brave, be bold
Be extreme, Alf was told,

By a chestnut intellectual
From Basel. So ineffectual
If you persist speaking so waspishly low
No one listens, they need the flow
That meaning teases. Words must plead
For Architecture to stay alive not bleed.
But really, with a message like yours
Hit the roof, go off walls and floors.
But so nice to see you so nice,
Glad you used the repetition device.

From Anyplace but here, Alf departed
Still unanswered visions uncharted.
Anyplane but this one, Go
Anyway it's really time, So
Alf, determined not to be the last
Modern Inaction Hero from the past,
Wrote, over the espresso, the third part
Beastly, horrid, straight from the heart:
Should he instead have stayed
In the bar where promise played?
And not idled so long at the bus stop
With that felt pen to review the crop
Of words scrawled on the walls
Of Architecture, along with *a load of balls*.

In between Alf made the Golden Gate,
The Sausalito Ferry forced to wait
For the weekend, the interview dragging
Through power breakfasts, American nagging
About Architecture with a capital A.
We expect you, of course, to work all day
And night, so a child you can forget
This is not a city in which to beget.

Surely this is something you don't mind?
Energy, speed, someone of the proactive kind
We seek to be our next Professor,
Not some tweeded, literary confessor.

On the Embarcadero, in The Hotel Griffon
Alf could no longer put any grip on
Architecture's vain and proactive greed,
Instead he hurried to the ferry at full speed.
Told himself, forget this scholar in residence
Europe always had this precedence.
So where were we, yes, Barcelona,
Alf very much the melancholy loner.
Exit the Colon out in Economy
Off to BA resisting the lobotomy,
Where in Aires we now return to look in on
Alf asleep in a borrowed condominium.

Potholed Corrientes way off to the east,
The Miami stuntman not in the least
Worried about breaking his vow
Enters, waking Alf saying: Now
Time for your first Argentinian Baby Beef
Which convinced Alf was coded golden leaf.

Morning came and coffee parted the two
Strangers, leaving Alf with that important few
Minutes before his lecture in the dark,
At Teatro Cervantes nearby the park
Where *El Conde* prowled as the Anti-Pole
You scum, you exile, you rant. His soul
Left high and dry outside Cafe Rex,
Now renovated into a Rapid Tex Mex.

At last, Teatro Cervantes all hushed and prepared
Velvet drapes, dudes and architects as if they cared.
At last, the lights flickered and dimmed
The poem took flight after being so heavy-limbed.
But out of the darkness and the gloom,
Out of the echoless harrowing room
At last, Alf cried, what is the use
Of Architecture's own game to deuce?
When the Endgame talked up and down,
Allows everyone to wear the crown
For fifteen minutes of near fame
Until swerving all in the same
Rise and Fall, but oh with such style;
Architecture pour rien will do for a while
Messieurs et mesdames, as a name
For the fated architectural frame.

And thus it was, Alf stuttered across
The beastly poem he thought might well toss
Out all Architecture's pretence and play
Until returning roundly to sense one day.
In the future, in the Gap. Without sorrow
An Architecture, in between today and tomorrow.

A numb thumb took Horrid Alf on again,
To part four, as far away from Spain
As possible under the circumstance
To Ithaca, Cornell, where by chance
The Global Positioning System found
The key under the mat safe and sound.
To the Peregrine House, feel free
Go right in, your room is two-O-three.
Through the fire door on the second
Landing, along the corridor that beckoned
Other tweeds, even Merton, up the stairs to climb
In the past long before Alf's time.

Make yourself at home, breakfast at eight
Eggs cooked but once, so don't be late.
And so by chance, by accident, by mishap,
In four days, Alf delivered *Mind the Gap*;
The working title of his forthcoming book
Which unfortunately was mistook
For the supplementary Beastly Poem
A sly attempt to swerve and throw them
Off the architectural nerve and scent
And a return of Alf's nausea prevent.

But it didn't and the vomit regularly hit
Before each lecture, tempting Alf to flit.
Eat the baby octopus, shrimps and snails,
The sushi, lobster and frog's tails.
And if anything should remain
Put it down to Global Migraine.

In Cornell, The Eagles were aired
Before their reunion, all was spared.
Welcome to The Hotel California played
Whilst the audience listened on, stayed.
The fourth part of the poem nigh finished
Voice even lower now, almost diminished.
Which left the Quintet, the fifth and last
In remembrance of architectural things past.
Thus repeated, doubtless all the same
Ditto Architecture, the name of the game.
Until it came and went so easily
A flashback to India, the stomach queasily
Upset, thrown off with that famous Delhi belly
Seen so ofen, bursting out of the telly.
In and out of gumbooted Thamescote, fall
An unnumbered Georgian haven on The Mall
Under the flight path, near the magnolia tree
Erskine's Ark, Heathrow's One, Two, Three.

Amoebic dysentery wasn't so easily treated
Alf divorcing, felt zero in summer, defeated.
But back and forth to the nonsmoking airport
Put Alf in frame for the final resort.
Lonely it was with only Kathleen Battle
The aria lost to some freak from Seattle,
Where Nirvana swopped coats for the trip
Leaving the Three Tenors so regrettably hip
To Architecture, football, cuisine and composure
And the art of avoiding foreclosure.

What might have been is now an abstraction
Redeemed by the Software's interaction.
Only in the neon digital lounge
Do the Modernists begin to scrounge.
Only in a world of speculation,
Architects now make their reputation.

A second marriage left the Horrid Author better
To cope with Architecture's latest fetter.
So down the corridor we do not take,
Towards the ballroom, with all the fake
Leather sofas and on to the unopened door
The secret of the rose garden even more
Intact than ever.
The Dust? Ah clever!
To know the disturbance owes all
To dis-figured discourse's last call.

At last, the beastly poem now over,
Leaves you the reader in the clover
Searching for the fourth leaf and the rhyme
To redeem Architecture one last time.
In brogues, Docksides, Vagabond or Nike
You can check out of the Hotel any time you like,

But from Architecture you will never leave
Tug as you might at the Academy's sleeve.

Pause before you flame the griddle
Baby beef aside, listen to this riddle:
Before you take to the air again
Chewing-gum sky, stretched aflame,
Remember the Horrid Author is someplace gone
Unlearning non-entity, happy to alight upon
The ancient authors, to plunder and elegantly cull
For his next book, *The Architectural Bull.*